Marvelous
MURALS
You Can Paint

Marvelous
MURALS
You Can Paint

NORTH LIGHT BOOKS
CINCINNATI, OHIO

www.nlbooks.com

GARY
LORD
&
DAVID
SCHMIDT

A Note About Safety

The authors and publisher disclaim any liability for damages or injury resulting from the use of this information.

Marvelous Murals You Can Paint. ©2001 Gary Lord and David Schmidt. Manufactured in China. All rights reserved. No part of this book may be reproduced in any form or by any electronic or mechanical means including information storage and retrieval systems without permission in writing from the publisher, except by a reviewer, who may quote brief passages in a review. Published by North Light Books, an imprint of F&W Publications, Inc., 1507 Dana Avenue, Cincinnati, Ohio 45207. (800) 289-0963. First edition.

Other fine North Light Books are available from your local bookstore, art supply store or direct from the publisher.

05 04 03 02 01   5 4 3 2 1

Library of Congress Cataloging-in-Publication Data

Lord, Gary
Marvelous murals you can paint / Gary Lord, David Schmidt.--lst ed.
    p. cm.
    Includes index.
    ISBN 0-89134-969-3 (alk. paper)
    1. Mural painting and decoration--Technique. I. Schmidt, David II. Title.
ND2550 .L67 2000
751.4--dc21
                    00-037236

Editor: Nicole Klungle and Maggie Moschell
Designer: Stephanie Strang
Cover designer: Stephanie Strang
Production artist: Donna Cozatchy
Production coordinator: Sara Dumford

Photo credits

The Finish Line, Trumbull, CT: page 6.

Ron Forth Photography, Boulder, CO: pages 7; 13; 82; 83 (bottom); 94; 95 (top and bottom left); 105; 106; 141 (bottom).

Robin Victor Goetz Photography, Dayton, KY: pages 27 (top); 33 (top); 37 (all); 84; 85; 121 (bottom right); 141 (top left).

Gary Lord: pages 74 (both); 96; 107.

Gary McCauley Photography, Cincinnati, OH: pages 2 (all); 3; 5; 9 (all); 11; 18; 27 (bottom); 28; 29; 33 (bottom); 34; 35 (both); 49 (both); 50 (both); 51 (all); 52; 53 (bottom); 57; 58; 60; 64; 67 (all); 68; 73; 75 (both); 76; 83 (top); 108-119; 120 (all); 121 (all); 122-139 (all); 140.

J. Miles Wolf, Wolf Photographic Arts, Cincinnati, OH: pages 73; 95 (bottom right); 107 (bottom); 141 (top right).

ABOUT THE AUTHORS

David Schmidt

After graduating from the Central Academy of Commercial Art in 1982, Dave moved to Chicago and worked as an Art Director for a large advertising agency. There he worked on both print and TV ad campaigns.

Dave moved back to Ohio in 1985. While looking for work in advertising, he worked part-time for Wall Options with Gary Lord. After a short time, he realized that he found this work far more enjoyable than advertising and went to work full-time for Gary.

In June of 1994, Dave started his own business, Classic Compliments, in Dayton, Ohio. In 1995, Dave and Gary opened Prismatic Painting Studio. They have since expanded and now teach classes nationally and internationally.

Dave has also contributed articles to The Artist's Magazine and Decorative Artist's Workbook.

Dave is very proud of this book and his other achievements over the past fourteen years and is looking forward to the next fourteen.

Acknowledgments

To my parents, Helena and Clifford Reusch. A special thanks to Julie, Sarah and Robert Lollar for their unending support and encoiuragement. To a very special person in my life, Pam Tinkham, and her children, Bret, Ali and Lauren.

Gary Lord

Gary Lord received a BFA from Ohio State University in 1974. In 1975 he opened Gary Lord Wall Options & Associates in Cincinnati and is still creating the whole spectrum of decorative paint finishes on a national and international level. Gary is also a co-owner of Prismatic Painting Studio with David Schmidt, where they both teach all forms of decorative painting techniques. They have taught thousands of students throughout the United States, Canada and in Europe. Gary has been a contributing editor for Decorative Artist's Workbook since 1992 and writes articles for other national and international painting and decorating magazines. Gary has appeared on the internationally syndicated Home and Garden Television Network, on Home Matters on the Discovery Channel and on many regional and local television and radio programs.

Acknowledgments

I wish to thank my wife Marianne and my children Ben, Corrie and Jared for their support and love in all aspects of my life.

I wish also to thank my fellow artists who helped us on some of the great murals shown in this book: Sandra Bakie, George Kitta, Victor Kurry, Kathleen Lichtendahl, Amy Overman, Helen Ryan, Mike Schmidt, Joe Taylor, Bill Turner, Sharon Culham, Micah Ballard, and Willard Collier.

Thank you also to the photographers who helped with all the beautiful photography: Gary McCauley, Robin Goetz, Ron Forth and J. Miles Wolf. Thank you also to all the clients that have generously allowed us to photograph their homes.

I want to also thank Benjamin Moore Paints and Aqua Finishing Solutions, loyal sponsors of many of our projects throughout the years.

Dedication

WE WOULD LIKE TO DEDICATE THIS BOOK TO OUR PAST,

PRESENT, AND FUTURE CLIENTS, WHO STILL BELIEVE IN

AND SUPPORT THE ARTS. WE WISH TO ALSO SAY THANK

YOU TO ALL OF THE WONDERFUL FRIENDS WE HAVE MET

THROUGH OUR TEACHING, ESPECIALLY THE MEMBERS OF

THE STENCIL ARTISAN'S LEAGUE, INC. AND THE NATIONAL

SOCIETY OF DECORATIVE PAINTERS.

TABLE OF CONTENTS

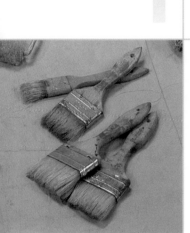

part

3

Projects

Introduction

We are very excited and pleased with what this book has to offer. Our goal was to write a concise but complete mural-painting book that would enable the reader to go from the most basic mural style to more advanced work. Each chapter builds upon the material in the previous chapters, so by the time you reach the more advanced projects, you will have a solid foundation for achieving the more challenging techniques.

In part 1 you will learn the importance of room preparation and the types of ladders and scaffolding that we as professionals feel are the best to use. We will also discuss drawing tools, spray equipment, brushes, rollers and paints. With the information in this section you will be able to select the right equipment and correct paints to paint any mural any size, anywhere.

In part 2 we explains how to choose the subject matter for your murals and how to acquire reference materials for developing your design from thumbnail sketches to full-color mock-ups. We will also cover color theory, how to make colors work for you and how colors create a mood. You will learn step by step how to use perspective drawing to add dimension to your work. We will also discuss composition and the uses of symmetrical, asymmetrical and radial balance. Following that, you will learn to enlarge and transfer your beautiful designs using four different methods that the professionals use. They are so easy to do and so quick, other people will think you are cheating.

In part 3 we will show you how to go from the most elementary style of mural painting to more complex and detailed murals. The first projects are two simple, but stunning, silhouette murals.

The next chapter builds on silhouette style often used in children's rooms. You will see how adding shadows and highlights gives more dimension and sophistication to your murals.

The next project shows you how to enhance a room by adapting designs from fabric, wallpaper, carpet and furniture. You can copy part of the design, alter it to please your eye and then match the colors. This technique will show you how to create flow, balance and harmony throughout the room you're decorating.

Project four will show you how stencils can be useful, either as an entire mural or as one component in a mural that uses hand-painting techniques as well.

Project five shows two ways to create beautiful sky murals. You can use the knowledge you gain in this chapter when you wish to advance to the next level and use the skies and cloud techniques with landscape painting.

Project six shows you how to create the illusion of dimensional textures in your murals. The demonstration features a wood-grained door, a fieldstone wall and a vine with leaves. Adding a drop shadow behind these elements adds to the feeling of realistic depth.

If you want to bring the great outdoors inside, you will enjoy the last project in which you will learn to paint realistic landscapes with mountains, grass, rocks, waterfalls and cloud-filled skies. These very detailed step-by-steps will allow you to proceed at your own pace to this more advanced level of mural painting.

We hope that you will enjoy the galleries at the end of the chapters and at the end of the book and that your creative process will be inspired by the wide variety of murals we have painted as professionals.

Equipment & Materials

BEFORE YOU BEGIN PAINTING A MURAL, YOU MUST FIRST PREPARE THE ROOM TO PROTECT THE THINGS IN IT FROM DAMAGE. NEXT, THE WALL MUST BE PREPARED BECAUSE A GOOD, SOUND PAINT SURFACE WILL NOT ONLY ALLOW YOUR MURALS TO LOOK BETTER, IT WILL ALSO ALLOW THEM TO LAST LONGER.

THE IMPORTANCE OF HAVING THE RIGHT TOOLS AND KNOWING HOW TO USE THEM SAFELY AND PROPERLY WILL ALSO BE ADDRESSED. WE WILL COVER THE USE OF LADDERS, SCAFFOLDING, DRAWING TOOLS, SPRAY EQUIPMENT, BRUSHES AND ROLLERS AS WELL AS A VARIETY OF PAINTS. THIS KNOWLEDGE WILL HELP YOU FEEL COMFORTABLE PAINTING ANY MURAL ANYWHERE.

St. John the Baptist Church in Middletown, Ohio, is a good example of a combination of a sprayed sky at the top of the half dome and a brushed sky by the windows. We also did all the general painting, gold gilding and marbelizing. The smaller altar mural is a mosaic that was done in the 1800s.

ROOM

$\mathcal{B}$efore doing any painting, survey the area you are to be working in. Decide if any furniture, pictures, drapery, carpets or accessories should be removed from the room. The emptier a room is, the less likely anything will be damaged.

You will need to decide what type of ladders or scaffold, if any, will be required in the room.

We will only touch briefly on wall preparation, because many other books discuss in detail how to patch and repair walls before painting. (See *Recipes for Painted Surfaces: Decorative Paint Finishes Made Simple* by Mindy Drucker and Pierre Finkelstein.)

Look at all the walls closely with a bright light, preferably halogen, to see if there are any dings, dents, scratches or cracks that need to be patched, sanded and primed before

painting. Repairing any faults on your painting surface will ensure that they do not call attention away from your finished work. It is always best to fix problem areas first because correcting them after the fact would require repainting parts of the mural. Use a caulking gun to recaulk any trim that needs it before you mask out the trim. The caulk must be dry before taping out the trim.

Before fixing any wall imperfections, bring in dropcloths to protect the floor. Use a tape gun to mask around the baseboard and the tops of doors and windows to protect from paint spatters.

You can also use 2-inch (51mm) wide masking tape around your window and door edges to protect them from paint. Masking tape is useful, but can be left on the trim for only a

This room has been prepared for painting with a spray gun. The windows are covered in clear plastic, as is the fireplace, the door and the stairway banister. The floor is covered in drop cloths, and all other flat horizontal surfaces are also masked off. The outlet covers have been removed, and the vent has been closed.

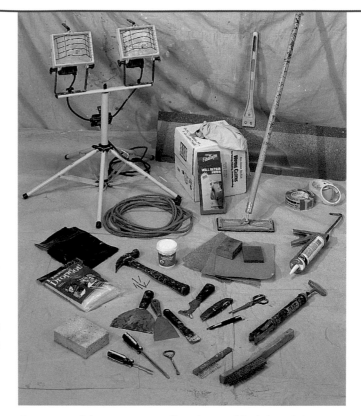

Some items useful in room prep are (from the upper left): halogen lights, spray shield, rags, wall repair kit, sanding pole, masking tape, electrical cord, garbage bags, spackle, sanding blocks and sandpaper, caulking gun, plastic dropcloths, hammer, finishing nails, hydrocellulose sponge, putty knives, utility knives, spinner (used for quickly drying paint brushes and rollers), screwdrivers, a paint opener and a wire brush.

few days or the adhesive may cause problems. If you are going to be on your project for a while, use blue tape, which will last seven to fourteen days even in direct sunlight.

If you are planning to spray paint in your room, you need to be a lot more careful than when using a brush or roller because of the overspray created by the spray gun. When masking out a room for a spray project, use 2-inch (51mm) wide masking tape and 4mil clear plastic to seal off the windows and doors. Cut the plastic to completely cover the door or window including the trim. Then use the masking tape to adhere the plastic to the trim, making sure the tape completely covers all the edges of the plastic and the outer edges of the trim.

A conventional cup gun creates a lot more overspray. If you are using a cup gun, cut a hole in the plastic in one window and put a fan in the window to evacuate the overspray as much as possible. Turn off or cover the heating and air conditioning vents in the room so the paint will not go through the HVAC system and get dispersed in other areas of the home. Finally, make sure that all the furniture and floor surfaces are totally protected before spraying.

PREPARATION

When you have removed everything possible, put down your dropcloths and masked out your trim, you can patch your walls if needed. Refer to the photograph on this page for a variety of tools to help you do this.

Your walls may just need a light sanding; use a pole sander for this. You may also need drywall mud to patch any dings or dents and sandpaper or sanding blocks to sand these patches smooth.

One note of caution: Any time you sand a drywall patch, a lot of dust is created. To keep this to a minimum, use sanding blocks wet with water. This keeps the volume of dust down tremendously.

Instead of a sanding block, you can use a slightly dampened hydrocellulose sponge. Rub it flat over the patched area in a

circular motion. Be careful not to rub too hard. The goal is to flatten out the patch so it is flush with the wall. If you rub too hard, you will remove too much of the patch itself and will wind up with a recessed area that you need to patch again.

You may find after using a damp sponge to smooth a patch that a "halo" of dried patching compound remains. To remove this, use a clean damp sponge to wipe the halo off right up to the edge of the patch.

After all the patches are sanded and all areas are caulked as needed, you are ready to apply a primer over your patches. If you have only a few patches, you can just prime those spots. However, if you have a lot of areas that have been patched, it is best to prime the whole wall.

LADDERS

S ince most murals cover a wall from top to bottom, you will need to stand on something to reach the upper wall or ceiling areas. Painters use step stools, stepladders, articulated ladders, extension ladders, scaffolding, stretch boards and ladder jacks for this.

It is important to buy a good-quality ladder that has an industrial rating suited to your height and weight. There are four main classifications for all stepladders and extension ladders: Class III (rated household) can support up to 200 lb. (90kg); Class II (rated commercial) ladders can support up to 225 lb. (101kg); Class I is heavy duty; and Class IA is an extra heavy duty rating to 275 lb. (124kg). With each classification the sturdiness and structural strength of the ladder increases, with Class III being the lightest and flimsiest and Class IA being very sturdy but heavy.

Ladders are made from aluminum, fiberglass or wood. Aluminum is the least sturdy and wood and fiberglass are of fairly equal strength. Aluminum ladders conduct electricity, so never, ever use them around electrical wiring, inside or outside. Wood ladders, if they have metal supports and brackets, can also conduct electricity. As time goes by, wood ladders will loosen up and get wobbly. They tend to collect moisture and swell or warp over time.

Fiberglass ladders, on the other hand, do not conduct electricity or warp. They are color coded for easy identification: red is for Class III household, green is for Class II commercial, blue is for Class I heavy duty, and orange is for Class IA extra heavy duty.

The chart shows 4-foot (1.2m) stepladders by classification and material and how much they weigh. Class III ladders are not recommended for a work environment because they simply aren't sturdy enough. We prefer either a Class II or Class I. The IA's get heavier as the ladder gets larger. On most jobs a 4- to 6-foot (1.2 to 1.8m) ladder is great. It can fit in most cars and trucks and is tall enough to reach most areas. Do not stand on the top step or platform. If you need to stand at a 4-foot (1.2m) height to reach something, you would need a 6-foot (1.8m) ladder.

If a stepladder will not reach your area, you may need scaffolding or extension ladders with a stretch board. We have scaffolding that is 29 inches (73.6cm) wide, 6 feet (1.8m) high and 6 feet long. Two of these can be stacked a maximum platform height of 12 feet (3.6m). The scaffolding has a guardrail for safety. A small collapsible scaffold, 18 inches (46cm) wide, 4 feet (1.2m) high and 4 feet long, is also useful. Scaffolds are nice because they can hold a lot of materials and still have room for the painter to stand and move about.

Extension ladders have a classification rating exactly the same as stepladders. They usually start at 16 feet (4.8m) and extend to 40 feet (12m), with increments of 4 feet (1.2m). If you use extension ladders for high areas, you will find them difficult to use by themselves. Instead, use two extension ladders and ladder jacks to hold a stretch board between them to walk or sit on. Ladder jacks come in two sizes, one that can hold a 14-inch (35.5cm) wide plank and one that can hold up to a 20-inch (51cm) wide plank. The stretch boards come in a variety of sizes and lengths. Aluminum is preferable because wood is springy, wobbly, and it warps. When you are standing on a 14-foot (4.2m) long plank 20 feet (6m) above the ground, you won't want to stand on a surface that wobbles.

Our favorite ladder is the Little Giant. It can do everything all the other ladders can, plus more. It can be an extension ladder, a stepladder, a stair ladder or an A-frame ladder. It is so versatile and sturdy, you probably won't need to buy anything more. We have abused this ladder for years and it keeps coming back every day for more. It's great!

LADDER WEIGHTS by type

Type	Aluminum	Fiberglass	Wood
II	9.5 lb.	10.5 lb.	15 lb.
I	10.5 lb.	13 lb.	19 lb.
IA	16 lb.	15 lb.	21 lb.

stretch board should be as level as possible. As you see, these can hold a lot of weight and are safe and sturdy to work on.

The photo on the left shows the scaffold we use most frequently in our work. Scaffolding, like ladders, comes in various sizes. The one that works for us 95 percent of the time is a system that has 29-inch (73.6cm) wide and 6-foot (1.8m) tall end frames. These are held erect by side rails that are 5 feet (1.5m) long. So, one scaffold rig is 29 inches (73.6cm) wide and 6 feet (1.8m) tall plus 8 inches (20cm) for the height of wheel casters and 5 feet (1.5m) in length. You can stack one system on top of another as shown in the photo to create a platform height of 12 feet (3.6m). When stacking scaffolding, it is required to have a guard rail system on the top section for additional protection.

One word of caution regarding scaffolding and stretch boards: Think! If people get hurt when using these systems, it's not because of system failure, but because of human error. People get hurt because they forget where they are after working six to eight hours and walk right off the stretch board. Sometimes people try to use the system in ways it wasn't designed to be used. Do not

SCAFFOLDING

*I*t seems that a lot of people want murals in areas difficult to access with a regular stepladder, such as stairways or high-ceilinged areas. Look at the murals of the White House Inn on this page and St. John the Baptist Church on page 13 and you will see that they could only have been done with special equipment.

In a stairwell, the Little Giant ladder is of great use. As you can see in the photo on page 17, the Little Giant ladder has expandable and retractable legs. This allows you to have a longer leg on a lower step of the stairway. For the next step, an extension ladder or tall stepladder can be used. In this case we used an extension ladder that braced against the lower step so the ladder could not kick out away from the wall. We used an aluminum stretch board to span between the Little Giant and the extension ladder. The

walk on the outside of the scaffolding and use only the end frames to climb up and down. Brace ladders securely into steps as we have shown, or tie them into a handrail or something sturdy so that the ladder cannot slip. If used carefully, these systems are safe. If you do not wish to purchase these items, you can rent them at a local tool supply company.

As you can see, this mural for the White House Inn in Cincinnati, Ohio was in a stairwell. We used the Little Giant ladder, a stretch board and an extension ladder here.

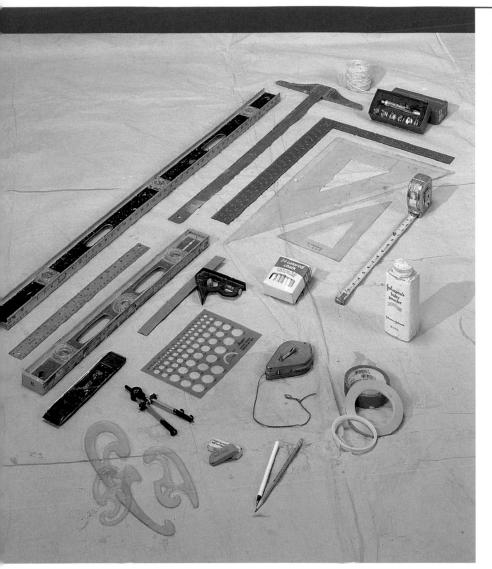

DRAWING TOOLS

*Y*ou will need a variety of tools to help you through the process of designing and laying up your mural. A good pencil, various triangles, a compass, French curves, a circle guide, drafting tape and erasers (not that we ever need erasers, mind you) help in drawing the original design and enlarging it for your final mural.

We use three different sizes of levels, a 25-foot (7.5m) measuring tape, a yardstick and two different squares, all of which help make sure the objects in the mural are level and square and that the perspective is correct. (Refer to the section on perspective for more information on these tools.)

String and a chalk box are used to lay up the horizon line. Chalk and artist's charcoal are used to draw a design on a wall because they can be easily painted over or wiped off with a dry or damp cloth. If you use a color of chalk close to the wall color, you won't be able to see it when the mural is finished. Pen, pencil and markers take many coats of paint to cover up, if they can be covered at all. This hinders you, especially if you want a loose, translucent, watercolor feeling in your final mural.

The Beugler striping tool is used to outline a graphic shape, such as the clown on page 68. See page 66 for a demonstration of using this handy tool. It is perfect for efficiently and neatly painting a long string of vines.

The cup gun and touch-up gun require an air compressor. The one shown here is a 5 hp model, which can put 100 pounds per square inch (psi) of compressed air into the hose. You can then regulate this with a valve on your cup gun. We usually spray with about 40 psi of pressure. You can further adjust the amount of paint and air that is sprayed out of the gun in both the HVLP and the cup guns by attachments on the spray guns themselves.

SPRAY EQUIPMENT

*I*n the photograph above you can see a variety of the spray guns and accessories we use.

There are three main types of spray equipment used in painting murals: the HVLP, the artist airbrush and the conventional cup gun. HVLP stands for high velocity, low pressure. This type of spray equipment creates less overspray than the conventional cup gun, though you still need to protect all areas from overspray. With the HVLP you can work in the room for hours and not create a paint fog as you would with the cup gun. If there is a downside to the HVLP, it's that you cannot attain as fine a line of spray as with the cup gun, and the spray is slightly grainier than with a cup gun or touch-up gun. All HVLPs will come with a 25- to 50-foot (7.5 to 15m) hose, a spray gun and a turbine compressor, which is usually light in weight and easy to carry around. HVLP systems are also not as noisy as larger conventional compressors.

We use the airbrush when we want a much finer line than possible with the other sprayers. The airbrush is used in smaller areas because it does not have a very large spray fan and so covers a very small area at a time. Also it holds only a small amount of paint at a time. The others hold quarts of paint, but most airbrushes can hold only a few ounces.

When spraying in a room with a conventional cup gun, mask off the room to protect everything (see the section on room prep). Put a box fan in the window and seal around it with plastic to help vent the overspray to the outside. Always wear a respirator so you don't breathe in the overspray. When spraying a large area over your head, wear a pair of clear goggles to keep the paint from your eyes and a spray hood to protect your head.

Paint strainers are used to remove any large particles that may block your spray gun.

This is an auto touch-up gun, a type of cup gun. It sprays large areas with a fine (not grainy) spray. The bottle on the bottom holds paint, and a compressor forces air through the rubber tube into the spray nozzle. The paint and air mix and leave the nozzle in a fine spray. The trigger is at the top of the gun and is controlled with one finger.

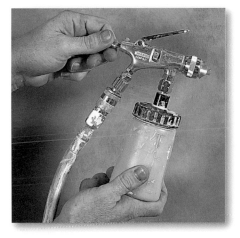

When using a spray gun, dilute your paint with water by 10 to 20 percent to allow it to flow through your gun better. Strain this mixture with a paint strainer, a nylon hose or with doubled-up cheesecloth as shown here.

You can adjust the rate of airflow and paint flow to create a variety of spray patterns. Less air and less paint gives you a small spray area. More air and more paint enlarges the spray area.

Always hold your gun 6 to 12 inches (15 to 30cm) away from the surface you are painting. Be sure to keep the gun at a 90° angle to the wall so that the spray hits the surface evenly. Keeping your spray gun parallel to the surface will prevent an uneven coat. You can fade color using a spray gun by shooting a dense pattern on one end and a lighter pattern on the other.

The right tool for the right job makes painting much easier and faster. A wide variety of fine art brushes and standard paint brushes and rollers are needed when painting a large mural. We also use sponges, rags, cheesecloth, steel wool—and, to clean up, Goof Off and rubbing alcohol.

BRUSHES AND ROLLERS

arge-scale murals require a variety of tools with which to apply the paint. The first tools you will use are paint rollers and paint trays for painting a basecoat on the wall as well as for blocking in large areas of your mural. You can use various roller sizes to fit the area you are painting.

Choosing a tool to fit the area is also important when selecting paint brushes. Often people who paint have their favorite brushes and like to use them all the time no matter what size the area is that they are painting. It is okay to use a ¼-inch (6mm) flat shader brush when doing the small limb work on a tree, but don't use that same size brush when painting a 12-inch (30cm) tree trunk. Time is valuable, so use the right size tool for the right area.

There are so many different types of brushes and manufacturers that you will have to experiment and play on your own to see what you like for different areas and techniques. We will suggest brushes for each project throughout the book.

Rags, sponges, steel wool, cheesecloth and many more objects can also be used to create beautiful textures in murals.

All the paint products used in this book are waterbased, so they clean up with soap and water while the paint is still wet. Be sure to clean your tools as soon as you are finished with them to avoid having the paint dry hard. Wash the tools in warm, soapy water and then rinse them clean.

We use a paint spinner to help clean and remove the paint from larger brushes and rollers. After you have cleaned artist's brushes, you can shape the brush and then put a little soap on the bristles. This will allow the brush to harden a little in its natural shape. (When you buy the brush new, it has sizing in its bristles to maintain its shape.) Store all your brushes in a brush holder, or stand them with the bristles up in a container as shown in the photo.

If paint does harden in your brush, you can save it by using a brush cleaner. Denatured alcohol, Goof Off, rubbing alcohol, lacquer thinner or a chemical brush wash will soften the dried latex paint. You can use a wire brush to remove the paint once it is soft. Then clean the brush and store it as mentioned above.

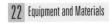

You can use a liner brush to create several different line widths by varying your pressure on the brush.

Light pressure with just the tip of the brush on the surface creates a thin line.

Heavy pressure, with almost the entire brush laying on the surface, creates the widest line.

By varying the pressure throughout one stroke, you can create a line that varies from thin to medium to heavy and back again. Use these techniques with a liner brush to outline shapes for 2-D graphics or when painting vines.

The acrylic paints are more brilliant in color and purity than latex emulsion paint, and they are also quite a bit more expensive than latex paints. A lot of the time we will use latex paints for larger areas (such as the sky, ground, etc.) and acrylics for details (such as animals or plants in the foreground).

Another way we use the latex paints is to buy what the paint manufacturers call a tinting base. Benjamin Moore makes five tinting bases for their paint. Each base is designed to enhance lighter or darker colors. This allows the manufacturer to mix up thousands of colors ranging from almost white to almost black. The difference between the bases is the amount of opaque white titanium dissolved in

PAINTS

$\mathcal{E}$very paint used in this book is a water-based product. We almost never use oil-based paints for murals because they dry slowly, they cannot be disposed of easily and are not user-friendly in terms of odor and clean up.

All paints consist of two basic parts: a base, such as latex, acrylic, lacquer or oil; and a colorant, which is a natural or synthetic pigment. The paint base acts as a binding medium, keeping the pigments bound to each other and to the painted surface. The pigments can be added to any type of paint base and mixed to create custom colors. You can purchase a paint base with the pigments mixed into it, or you can buy the base and the pigments separately and mix them yourself.

Types of Paint

In this book we use two types of water-based paints: latex and acrylic. Latex paint is a generic term for a wide variety of water-based dispersions of powdered pigments into a base of rubber or resin. Latex paints are available in pints, quarts, gallons and 5-gallon containers. They are also available in different sheen levels, from flat, satin and semi-gloss to high gloss.

Artist acrylic colors are made from powdered pigments ground into acrylic polymer resins. They are packaged in tubes or jars from 2 oz. to 1 gallon (60ml to 3.8l) and often have a creamy consistency that can be thinned with water.

the clear base. The lighter the color you want, the greater the amount of titanium in the base. The darkest colors are mixed with the darkest base, which contains no titanium at all. The opacity and whiteness of the titanium allow colors with a very small amount of pigment to be applied with the same coverage as paints with a lot of pigment in them. More colorant is needed for darker colors, but the colors are more translucent because the base carries less titanium. The amount of titanium in the base also affects the drying time of the paint: high-titanium bases dry faster than titanium-free bases. Please note that you cannot use a pigment or colorant by itself as pure paint—or even in a mix containing 90 percent colorant. Pigments will not set or adhere to a surface unless mixed with sufficient binding material—in this case, the paint base.

The advantage to purchasing a paint base and separate universal colorants is flexibility. With your own tint base and several colors of pigment, you can mix any amount of any color for yourself—you don't have to buy a quart of every color in your mural.

We mix up most of our colors in 12-oz. (360ml) plastic cups and label them with the color name and where it is used. Dave uses a plastic glove to seal the mouth of the cup each night so the paint doesn't dry out.

Large plastic buckets are good to hold water to rinse your brushes. A hair dryer is also great to use for drying down your wet color to see what the dry color looks like. All water-based colors are a little lighter in value when wet than when they dry. A rule of thumb is if the color matches perfectly when it is wet, it will be too dark when it is dry.

Glazes

In the chapter on creating realistic textures, we demonstrate methods of glazing, applying layers of opaque and transparent paint in succession. Glazes are transparent layers of darker colors applied over lighter ones, and scumbles are transparent layers of lighter colors applied over darker ones. Color resulting from this type of application has a greater luminosity than can be achieved with just opaque painting. This is because light is not only reflected from the surface of the paint film but also travels through the paint and is refracted and reflected from the paints underneath. Therefore a strong hue such as red-orange can be softened and made to appear cooler by glazing over it with a transparent blue.

When you are planning to use a glaze, paint your mural lighter and more sharply detailed than you intend it to be in the end. Glazing and scumbling will lower the value and brilliance of the color and obscure detail to a certain degree. There are three ways that we make glazes and scumbles in this book. The first is by adding water to the paint, which dilutes it, makes it more transparent, and lightens its value. The paint also loses some of its brilliance. (See the color theory section for a chart on this.)

The second method is to add colorant to a translucent glazing medium, such as AquaCreme by Aqua Finishing Solutions. This is a glazing medium that you can tint with 100 percent acrylic or universal colorant. AquaCreme is also an extender, which means you will have a longer working time to blend your paints. Sometimes we will add it to our paint as a retarder and blending medium to help us create subtle shades of color. (Note the shading of the clown and the blended sky in the silhouette project.)

The third method of creating glazes and scumbles is to add latex or acrylic paint to a clear base. AquaGlaze by Aqua Finishing Solutions is a clear medium that is added to latex paint to create a translucent, slower-drying paint. We usually mix 75 percent AquaGlaze with 25 percent latex paint. This allows us a longer working time with our glazes or scumbles.

Mix small amounts of your paints in plastic cups and label each cup with what the paint was used for.

Seal each cup with a plastic glove between uses.

Applying a glaze coat.

Applying scumble.

part 7

Preparing Your Design

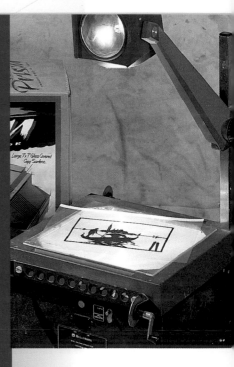

THIS SECTION OF THE BOOK WILL GUIDE YOU THROUGH THE PROCESS OF CREATING A MURAL. YOU WILL LEARN HOW TO CHOOSE YOUR SUBJECT MATTER, OBTAIN REFERENCE MATERIAL, AND CREATE THUMBNAIL SKETCHES AND COLOR MOCK-UPS OF YOUR MURAL. YOU WILL ALSO FIND INSTRUCTION IN COLOR THEORY AND HOW HUE, VALUE, INTENSITY AND COLOR TEMPERATURE CAN HAVE A LARGE IMPACT ON YOUR FINAL MURAL. THE IMPORTANCE OF PERSPECTIVE WILL ALSO BE ADDRESSED. THE SECTION ON PERSPECTIVE WILL SHOW YOU HOW TO MAKE YOUR MURALS REALISTIC BY THE PROPER USE OF ONE- AND TWO-POINT PERSPECTIVE. YOU WILL ALSO DISCOVER HOW COMPOSITION CAN CREATE A MOOD OR FEELING IN A PAINTING BY THE ARRANGEMENT OF OBJECTS, COLOR, TEXTURE, SHAPE, SPACE, LIGHT AND LINE. THEN YOU WILL BE READY TO ENLARGE AND TRANSFER YOUR DESIGNS TO THE SURFACE OF YOUR CHOICE, USING ONE OF FOUR DIFFERENT METHODS.

SUN
AND
WAVES
BEFOR
OVERSPRAY

...TER

...RFACE
...ATER

...TER

...D RANGE
...ND OVER
...SPRAY

...TER

...K BASE
...ND "

SAND

SAND HIGH LINE

This is a small-scale, full-color mock-up of a mural. It's a good idea to make one of these prior to starting the full-scale project.

With the help of your reference photos or clip file, rough pencil drawings, known as thumbnails, can be drawn. Once you are pleased with the general idea and layout, it is extremely helpful to make a color mock-up before getting started on the full-scale mural.

CHOOSING
A SUBJECT

The exciting thing about painting a mural is that it can be of anything you want. You can choose a cute whimsical theme for a child's room such as a collage of your child's favorite sports, animated characters, or rainbows and unicorns. You might want to have a soft, restful mural of one of your favorite vacation areas, which could be an ocean scene, mountains with waterfalls, a French countryside or a peaceful meadow with deer. The possibilities are endless. By looking through the many different murals and the variety of styles and themes in this book, you will have some help in deciding what type of mural you would like to have. Also, look through other books, magazines or personal photographs to help you select your subject matter. The public library is a great reference source.

Once your major subject is selected, let's say a Northwestern mountain scene, you will need to narrow in on the details that you wish to include in the mural. You may love waterfalls and lakes, so let's include that somehow. Perhaps different types of rocks and their formations always captivate your soul. Don't forget the big, gorgeous skies with beautiful cumulus cloud formations. Northwestern ponderosa pine trees with various indigenous wildflowers and plants add a

This is just a portion of our clip file of reference photos that have been pulled from magazines on a wide variety of subjects. It is a good idea to continuously add to your clip file and to organize your clippings into subjects, such as animals, skies, rocks, clouds, etc.

When working on your mock-up, keep a record of every color you use. Although you may choose to change these colors later, keeping a record such as this one will save you hours in the long run.

good color balance. Animal life such as eagles, elk, mountain goats and raccoons give you a center of interest. Once you have decided which elements you want, it is time to combine them into a thumbnail sketch.

Not many people are able to draw all of these elements without some form of reference material. No matter if you want to paint one mural or ten, a reference file is essential. Shown here are pictures torn from magazines or personal photographs, broken down into categories. These are an invaluable resource, not only for composition, but also for different light sources, varying seasons, perspectives, values, colors and more. From the montage of resource material you can start to make your thumbnail sketches.

Thumbnail sketches are quick drawings that allow you to start to establish your composition, including color values and perspective. Once you are pleased with your sketch, you can move on to a color mock-up of the thumbnail design.

The color mock-up is where you really finalize your composition, your color palette (see the section on color theory), your color values, temperature and brilliance of your painting. If you do a color mock-up before you start your full-size mural, many potential problems will be resolved before starting the job. If you do the color mock-up first, you can keep a record of all the colors you used for each area of the mural as shown on this page. You will find that a color mock-up for a silhouette is not as essential as it is for a more detailed realistic mural. But it never hurts to have as much figured out as possible before beginning to paint your actual mural.

Color wheel labels (clockwise from top):
- red — PRIMARY
- red-orange — TERTIARY
- orange — SECONDARY
- yellow-orange — TERTIARY
- yellow — PRIMARY
- yellow-green — TERTIARY
- green — SECONDARY
- blue-green — TERTIARY
- blue — PRIMARY
- blue-violet — TERTIARY
- violet — SECONDARY
- red-violet — TERTIARY

There are twelve hues on a color wheel: three primary colors, three secondary colors, and six tertiary colors.

Hue

Hue is the color name: red, yellow, blue, orange, etc. There are three primary colors that cannot be mixed from other colors. These are red, yellow and blue. These primary colors form the basis for the color wheel and from these three colors you can mix all other hues. The color wheel establishes logical relationships useful in color mixing and design, so get to know it well. As each color moves toward the next on the color wheel, it assumes the traits of its neighbors.

Between the primary colors are three secondary colors: green, violet and orange. These are mixed from the primary colors. By mixing any secondary color with the primary on either side of it on the color wheel, you get a tertiary color.

Notice that the primary and secondary colors are described with one word: red, yellow, orange, etc. The tertiary colors are described with two words: blue-green, red-violet, etc.

COLOR THEORY

C olor is one of the most exciting art elements. It can create an entire mood, whether it be bright, bold and energetic, or quiet, somber and reflective. Color theory is very complex and to really understand it can be a lifelong endeavor. As in most things in life, there are guidelines in color theory that will help achieve better success more often than not, if followed correctly.

These few short pages could never begin to explain the depth of color theory, but perhaps your curiosity is piqued enough that you will practice some of these techniques and explore color for yourself.

The first word is the adjective that describes the dominant hue of the color. Therefore, blue-green is a green color that's a little more blue than basic green. All of these colors make up the twelve hues on a color wheel. Understand that hue and color are general terms only and that pigment and paint names are very specific. Although there are only twelve hues on the color wheel, there are hundreds of pigment and paint variations of every hue. Colors will be described in this book by their hue name, pigment name, paint name or a number.

Be careful when using paints that have the same names but are made by different manufacturers, because there may be variations in the pigments used.

One last comment on hues—you may have noticed there is no mention of black, white or gray yet. These are considered to be colorless or achromatic. All other hues are called chromatic. When you mix a pure color with white, you get a tint; mix a color with gray, and you get a tone; mix a color with black, and you will get a shade.

Three-step value scale

Value

Value means the darkness or lightness of a color. A value scale is a ten step gradation of any color that shows the color as it moves from light to dark. A tint moves toward white and a shade moves toward black. Yellow is the lightest color and violet is the darkest on a standard color wheel. Painter Jo Sonja Jansen once compared the value scale to a ten-step staircase coming up from a dark basement. At the top of the stairs the sun is shining, and at the bottom of the stairs it's completely dark. As you ascend from the basement you step on stair one or value one, and it gets a little lighter. Then you step on stair two or value two and it gets even lighter. As you continue to ascend the ten steps or values, you gradually go from dark to light.

Look at the ten-step value scale and note how soft and easy the transition of color is for your eye to follow. The five-step scale contains every other value from the ten-step scale. Even though it is missing every other color, your eye still makes an easy transition from values one to nine. This happens because values that are no farther apart than two values can be blended easily with the eye. The three-step value scale shows what happens if there's more than a two-value gap between colors. Your eye jumps across the colors for a much stronger contrast. If you get your values wrong in a painting, the elements will appear to jump out at you.

For example, say you are painting a beautiful landscape and you want the fox drinking from the stream to be the focal point, but the waterfall in the distance behind the fox is all that you see. Most likely you haven't stepped your values correctly. Graduating your values means a gradual transition. Your darkest values should be in the foreground, then mid values, and finally your lightest values in the background. This can all change, however, because of the placement of your light source—such as placing the moon behind the mountain in the wolf mural on page 33. Atmospheric perspective is the term for how the values of colors lighten up and turn blue as the objects recede further and further into the background.

Five-step value scale

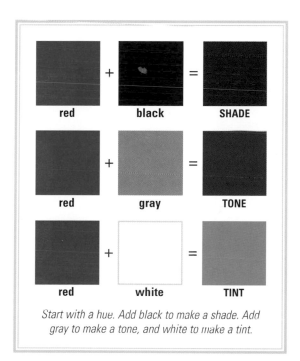

Ten-step value scale

red	+	black	=	SHADE
red	+	gray	=	TONE
red	+	white	=	TINT

Start with a hue. Add black to make a shade. Add gray to make a tone, and white to make a tint.

How Hue and Value Relate

Here is a tip that many artists use to see values: squint your eyes when you look at a color. This allows you to see the value of the paint more than the exact hue. The scale on the right, below, shows that different hues can have the same value. The scale next to it shows that you can also change the value of a color by increasing its translucence. In this case watercolors were used, so water was added to the color. You can also do this with acrylic or latex paints. For oil-based paints, just add paint thinner to increase the translucence. The last scale shows a full value scale in green which was made by starting out with value five and adding white to values six, seven, eight and nine and black to values four, three, two and one.

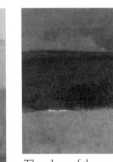

Decreasing value by increasing translucence

Three hues of the same value

A full value scale made by adding black to values below five and white to values above five

The column of colors on the left is a value scale using a hue mixed with white. The value of each color across the rows is very similar. However, each column is of a lower intensity than the column to its left because it contains a higher proportion of gray.

According to the most general rules of atmospheric perspective, colors lighten and acquire a blue cast as they recede into the distance. Brighter and darker colors are used in the foreground (below). However, placement of your light source can affect the arrangement of values in your mural. In the wolf mural (left) the location of the moon behind the mountain determines that the darkest value be used in the background and the lightest in the foreground.

Intensity

Oftentimes people are confused by intensity and value. Remember that value is the lightness or darkness of a color. Intensity of a color, sometimes called brilliance or chroma, refers to a color's brightness or dullness. A pure bright color has a high intensity while a grayed color has a low intensity. The extreme of low intensity is a neutral gray.

By using color intensity in a variety of ways, you can control compositional emphasis and create a setting for beautiful color effects. For instance, when mixing two adjacent high intensity colors, the mixture will slightly lower in intensity than either color by itself. You will notice the greatest decline in intensity when the two colors are far apart on the color wheel. Lower a bright color's intensity by mixing in black, gray or an earth color. Note: It is very difficult, if not impossible, once you have lowered a color's intensity to turn it back into a pure hue again. In the color chart on page 32, there is a vertical value scale from light to dark on the left. Only white was used to change the value. In the next row a small amount of gray was added to the colors, matching the value level as closely as possible. For the next row more gray and less color was added, again matching the value as closely as possible. This continues across the rows until the final colors are mostly gray with only a hint of the original color.

Temperature

The fourth and final component of color is temperature. As you look at the color wheel on page 30, you can see that half of the colors are warm (red-violet to yellow) and half are cool (violet to yellow-green). Color temperature helps create mood, depth and movement, and thus adds to the realism of your painting. Warm colors advance and cool colors tend to recede. This can be seen in the mural on this page, which has a lot of cool colors in the background and foreground. The warm red flowers "pop" off the cooler colors.

Color temperature is relative. A color that appears warm in one place may look cool in another depending on how it is used with its surrounding colors. Every color has many temperature variations, so practice will help you see the differences. Highlights are places where there is the highest concentration of light on an object (such as sunlight on mountain tops). The sun is warm, as are most highlights. But there are also cool highlights, such as violet highlights on snow on an overcast wintry day. Colors in shady areas tend to be cool. But if objects are reflecting warm light into the shady area, the shadows may tend to be on the warm side.

To create a strong sense of depth in your paintings, carefully monitor color temperature. To warm up a color, you would add any color that's warmer than the initial color. It is best to add a relat-

Notice that the red flowers, which are warm colors, "pop" off the background of blues and greens, which are cool colors.

ed color. If you were using violet, you could add red to warm it up. To cool a color you would add a color that is cooler than what you were using. If you were using yellow-green, add more green. Red-orange is the warmest color and blue-green will be your coolest.

On the color wheel (page 30) the hues opposite each other are called color complements. One color is a warm color and the other one is a cool color. This is important to know because if you mix a little of a color's complement into itself, you will decrease or reduce its color intensity.

This mural is painted primarily in two values of blue, which is a monochromatic color scheme.

Color schemes

Color schemes are based on a dominant color. Monochromatic schemes are based upon one color in different values. Analogous schemes are based upon colors that are adjacent on the color wheel. Split complementary color schemes are composed of three colors: one color and the two on either side of its direct complement.

There is an enormous amount of information about color theory that has not been covered here. Further reading is advisable. Practice, practice, practice to understand the subject more clearly. If you want to learn to make colors, get a paint deck from your paint supplier that lists the formulas of the universal tints and the base color for each color. Then buy the universal tints and the base colors and custom-tint your colors to match the paint chips.

This mural shows an analogous color scheme.

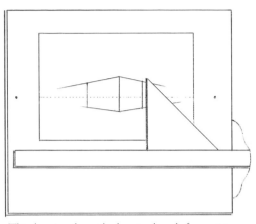

David is prepared to draw in precise perspective with straightedges, a triangle, masking tape, a pencil and posterboard.

This drawing shows the drawing board of an artist with a triangle, T-square and paper. Note that the vanishing points are off the paper.

PERSPECTIVE

*P*erspective is a technical skill that has rules. Anyone can do a quality perspective drawing once the rules are learned. Perspective makes the objects we draw look solid and gives them dimension. Strong skills in perspective will improve your ability to paint excellent murals.

We will look at two types of perspective: one-point and two-point (based on the number of vanishing points in the drawing). Both are easily mastered and are the basic framework for drawing almost anything in perspective. All objects in a mural appear smaller as they approach the vanishing point, and larger the closer they get to the viewer.

One-point perspective works well when it is viewed from one specific spot. For example, if a hallway wall mural is going to be most often viewed from one end of the hallway, one-point perspective will work well.

Two-point perspective gives a more realistic dimensional quality to murals and requires more steps to complete. In one-point perspective the vanishing point is usually located on the drawing surface. In two-point perspective, the vanishing points are often located outside the bounds of the drawing, which makes it more challenging.

For these exercises in perspective, you will need: a large piece of paper, pushpins, a pencil, a T-square, an eraser, drafting tape and a clear plastic triangle. When drawing a horizontal line, rest a T-square firmly against the straight edge of your desk or table. When drawing a vertical line, rest a triangle firmly against your T-square. When connecting one line to another, such as the corner of a box, the lines must connect precisely. If not, your drawing will not line up properly.

When drawing in perspective on a wall, place your horizon line at the eye level of the viewer, 5'5" to 6' (1.6-1.8m). Measure this and snap a chalk line. Use pushpins or nails for vanishing points. Finding a straightedge long enough to reach the vanishing points is impossible. Instead, tie string to the nails at the vanishing points and pull tightly to create a straight line from the vanishing points to the line you're drawing. Make several marks along the line and connect them with a straightedge. Use a level for an accurate vertical line. When the mural is complete, the holes can be patched and painted.

If your vanishing points extend beyond the corners of the wall, do a drawing to scale and use an overhead projector to transfer the image. It works, but you will have to make adjustments by eye because the projector tends to distort the image slightly.

With your newfound knowledge of perspective, your murals will take on a whole new dimension, pulling the viewer into your work.

When you know how to use perspective, you can achieve some stunning effects with your murals.

FAR LEFT PANEL ① ②

Let's start with the horizon line. The horizon line is a horizontal line that divides the sky from the ground. Where things sit in relation to the horizon line determines how we see it. If we place a box in front of us at eye level, we see only the side or sides of the box, not the top or bottom. We see distance by the overall size of common objects. Things appear smaller the farther away they are from the viewer. This is also true of space and distance. The car parked in your driveway appears much larger than a car parked a block away. Look at the spacing of telephone poles when you are traveling down a straight highway. The farther the poles are from the viewer, the smaller the space appears between each pole. This also applies to the spacing between parallel horizontal lines. As they recede, the visual distance between them is reduced. But by how much? If you follow the lines all the way to the horizon line, you will see they all meet at one point, the vanishing point

Now let's get started with an exercise in creating one-point perspective—that is, perspective using one vanishing point.

Where an object sits in relation to the horizon line determines how we see that object.

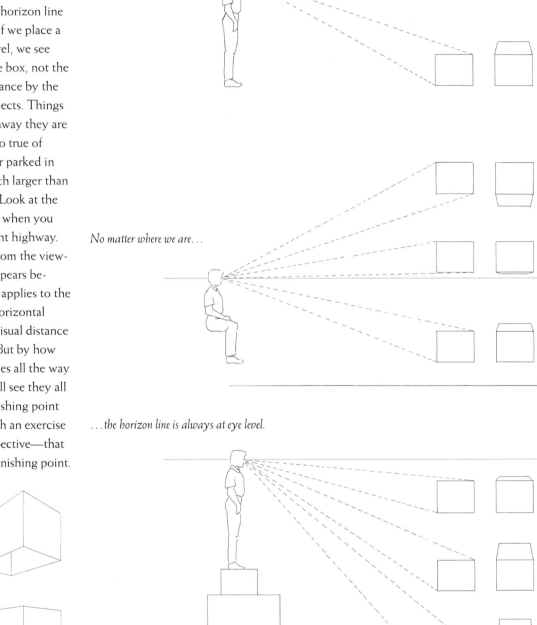

The horizon line is always at eye level.

No matter where we are…

…the horizon line is always at eye level.

1

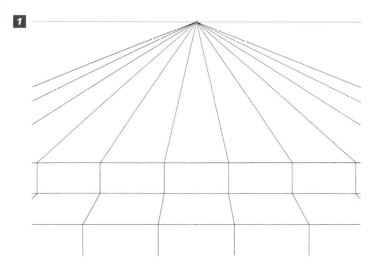

2

3

4

Figure 1 › As parallel lines recede, the distance between them is reduced.

Figure 2 › First and always first, place your horizon line. Since this is just a practice exercise, place your horizon line in the center of your paper. This is done using your T-square.

Figure 3 › Next, on the center of your horizon line, place a small dot. This is your vanishing point. The vanishing point is where receding parallel lines meet on the horizon line.

Figure 4 › With the base of your triangle set firmly against your T-square, draw a light center line down from your vanishing point. Use the vertical side of the triangle to draw the sides of a box, and slide the T-square to make the top and bottom.

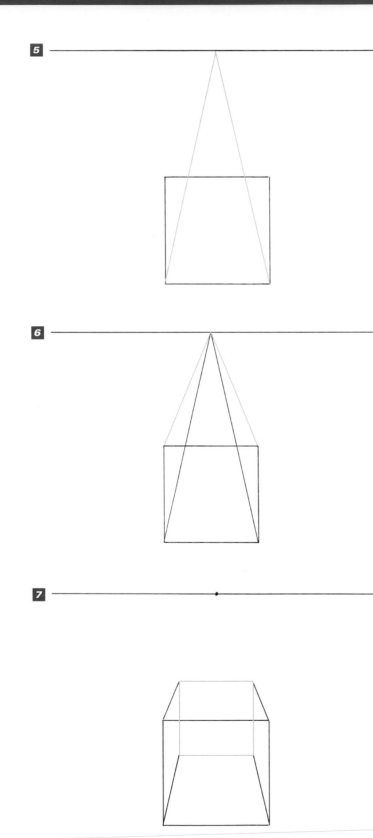

Figure 5 › Next, draw a line from the lower left and right corners of your square to your vanishing point. You can slide your T-square out of the way and use a straightedge to draw these lines.

Figure 6 › Now draw two more lines from the vanishing point to the top two corners of your box.

Figure 7 › You can see the square is taking on some dimension. To draw the back end of the box, another square is drawn with each corner touching the receding parallel lines. That's it! You have a box drawn in one-point perspective.

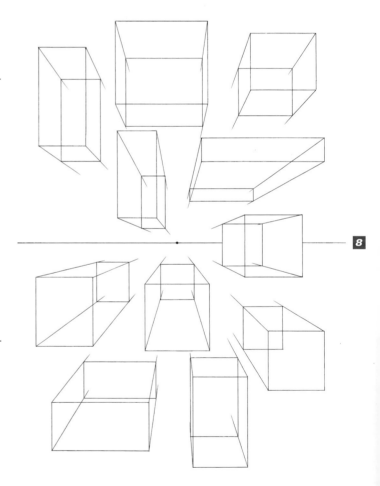

Figure 8 › From that one vanishing point, other boxes can be drawn. Notice the boxes above the horizon line. You can now see the bottom of these boxes. That's because any object above the horizon line is above our eye level. Practice one-point perspective by drawing boxes of different sizes and shapes using only one vanishing point.

Figure 9 › All the boxes in one-point perspective have something in common. They all face directly at you. To turn the box or angle it slightly, you need to use two-point perspective. To start, draw the horizon line.

Figure 10 › Next, draw the front vertical edge closest to the viewer. This is done using your triangle and T-square. It is important to remember that all vertical lines in one- and two-point perspective are just that: vertical. Vertical lines are not altered by perspective.

Figure 11 › Mark the horizon line directly above the vertical edge and measure out an equal distance from that point to locate your left and right vanishing points. Although you can put your vanishing points anywhere on the horizon, following these instructions will ensure that your drawing looks like mine.

Figure 12 › In two-point perspective, every line you draw will extend to either your left or right vanishing point, except for your vertical lines. › Now that the height of the box has been determined by the front corner (the vertical line) drawn earlier, draw a line from the top and bottom corners to your vanishing point right (v.p.r.). Repeat to vanishing point left (v.p.l.). › Hint: It will be easier and help your lines "click" if you use pushpins for your vanishing points. Your T-square can rest against them for a more accurate line.

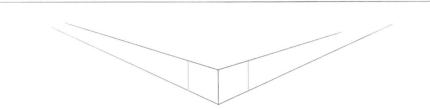

Figure 13 › To establish the width and length of your box, draw a vertical line on each side of the front corner, inside the lines extending to the vanishing points.

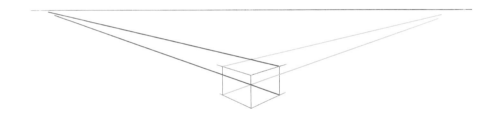

Figure 14 › Draw a line from the top and bottom of these two outside edges to the opposite vanishing point. Lines from the right vertical edge are drawn to vanishing point left; lines from the left vertical edge are drawn to vanishing point right. Where these two lines intersect on top and bottom determines the back vertical edge. Two sides of the box are now complete!

Figure 15 › Where the top and bottom lines intersect indicates where the back corner is located. This is a vertical line drawn in with your triangle and T-square. Now you will find out if all your lines click. (If your lines drawn earlier are off just a little, your back corner will not line up top to bottom.) Your box is complete.

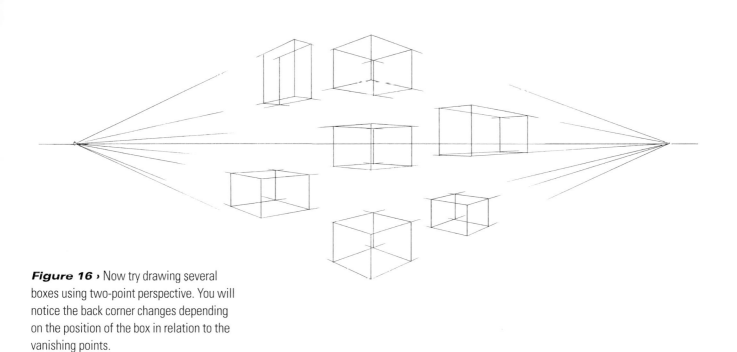

Figure 16 › Now try drawing several boxes using two-point perspective. You will notice the back corner changes depending on the position of the box in relation to the vanishing points.

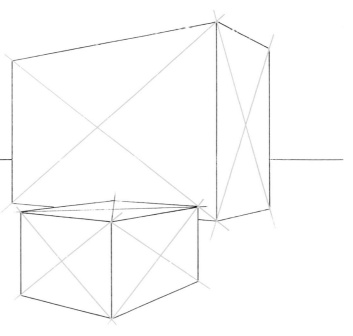

Figure 17 › When working in perspective, there will be times when you will need to locate the center of the side of a box. Since the box is drawn in perspective, simply measuring from the front corner to the back corner and dividing by two will not work. To accurately and easily find the center, draw diagonal lines from corner to corner. The center location of the side of the box will be where the two lines intersect.

Figure 18 › The key to drawing circles in perspective, such as the top of a wine glass, is to first draw a cube and locate its center. › Next, draw a vertical line intersecting the center. Then draw a line from v.p.r. through the center point as well. (If the circle faces right, draw the horizontal center line from v.p.r. If it faces left, draw it from v.p.l.) The side is now divided into eight equal parts. Do the same to the opposite side of the cube.

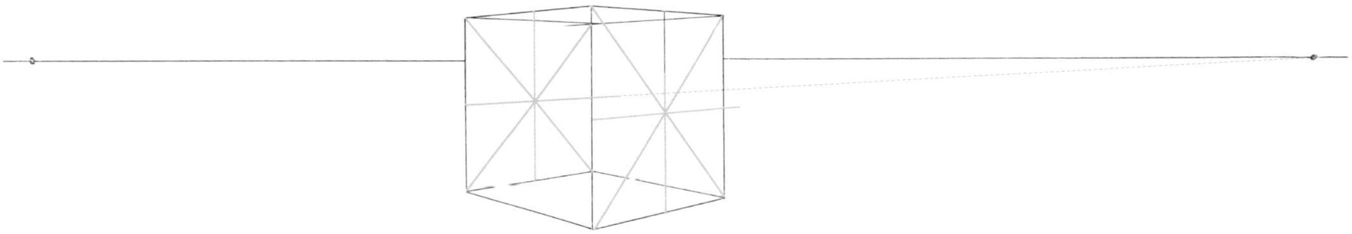

Figure 19 › To start your circle, draw a smooth arc in one quarter of the cube face. Use the intersection of the arc with the diagonal line as a starting point for a smaller square set inside the first. Use the vanishing point to establish the top and bottom of the square. The distance from the top line of the square to the middle line equals the distance from the middle to the bottom line. You can make the back square proportional to the front square by using the opposite vanishing point (in this case, v.p.l.) to draw lines from the corners of the smaller front square to intersect with the diagonals on the back cube face. The corners of the smaller back box are located where the lines intersect.

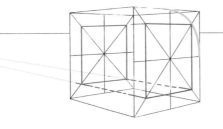

Figure 20 › Use these smaller squares as a reference point for drawing the rest of your circles. Now you have two circles drawn in proper perspective.

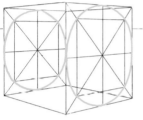

Figure 21 › Using v.p.l., conncct the top of the back circle to the top of the front circle. Repeat for the bottom of the circles, using the same vanishing point. You have drawn a cylinder. You will probably need to practice this exercise to master it.

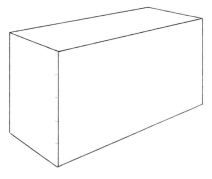

Figure 22 › You may need equal horizontal measurements in some drawings. For instance, you may want to draw a row of books. Start by determining how many equal horizontal segments you will need. Draw an extended box shape to the visual length you would like. Then mark the vertical front edge of your box with the number of horizontal segments you need, spacing them equally. Note: In this exercise, as will be the case with many murals, my vanishing points are located off the edges of the drawing surface.

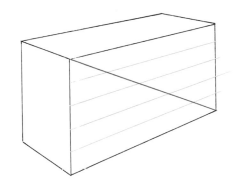

Figure 23 › Once again, remember that if you want your segments to face right, draw lines from v.p.r. If you want it to face left, draw from v.p.l. In this case, I want my segments to face right. Draw horizontal lines from the vanishing point through the tic marks you made on the front edge of the box. Then draw a diagonal line from corner to corner so that each line is intersected by the diagonal line.

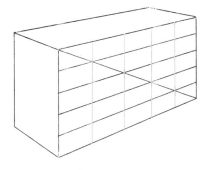

Figure 24 › Next draw a vertical line through each intersection, using your T-square to keep the lines vertical. Now you have equal segments drawn in perspective.

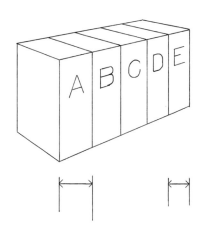

Figure 25 › Notice the difference between the width of the first box (A) and the last box (E), which is farther away.

Figure 26 › This living room scene was drawn using basic box shapes and circles in perspective.

Figure 28 › These round objects were drawn with box bases, circles, and cylinders.

Figure 27 › You can now see how each item was constructed from basic box shapes.

Figure 29 › Now you can see how each object started out as a box.

COMPOSITION

omposition is everything to a painting. It is the arrangement of objects, color, texture, shape, space, light and line. This arrangement can create a mood or feeling in a painting. Visit your local art museum and study the masters. Do you find the painting soothing and relaxing, happy or sad, exciting or frightening? Composition plays a part in all these emotions. A painting with poor composition will not hold the viewer's attention.

Liking or not liking a certain composition is a matter of taste, and as with anything in the world of art, nothing is written in stone. However, there are certain factors that affect how your eye travels through an image. This chapter will show you options in compositional design.

Let's start with how you see a painting. As you read the text in this book, you read from left to right. We read paintings the same way. We start at the left, if only for a split second, then begin to travel to the main focal point. The eye can be pulled quickly to the subject, or the composition can slowly pull us in. Once the eye locates the main focal point of the painting, it tends to wander. A good composition will direct the eye through the painting and back to the main focal point, locking the eyes of the viewer inside the picture.

As an artist works, you may notice him stop and stare at his painting. He may tilt his head, close one eye, and step back a distance. Why? Balance. You don't have to be an artist to see or feel it. If the painting has no balance, both the artist and viewer will sense something is not quite right.

There are three types of balance: symmetrical, asymmetrical and radial. When arranging your composition, keep it simple. Use only the elements that support your original idea. Unnecessary elements add nothing but confusion. Finally, use thumbnails—and lots of them—to work out any problems you may have with the composition.

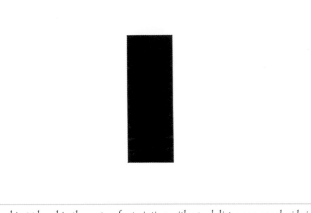

An object placed in the center of a painting with equal distance on each side is a good example of symmetrical balance. If the painting were divided in half, vertically, each side would have an equal amount of design as the other half.

Any object placed left or right of center will be balanced by the open or negative space across from the subject.

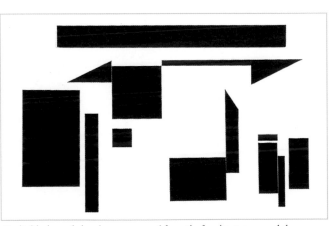

Radial balance helps the eye to travel from the focal point around the painting in a circular motion, returning again to the main focal point. The eye never leaves the picture.

Most compositions use both negative and positive space. Positive space is usually occupied by objects, the subjects of the composition. Negative space surrounds and balances the positive space.

Use of negative space is one way to pull the eye to the subject. The positive space in this composition is taken up by the tree and the owl.

Notice how the negative space creates "pointers" that go directly to the subject.

Contrast in color is a great way to pull the eye into the subject. Any dark color on light, or light color on dark, will quickly grab the attention of the viewer.

Shadows can also pull the eye into the subject. Even though the value of the tree is close to the value of the stormy sky, the shadow traveling across the foreground pulls you to it.

Compositions are vertical if they are taller than they are wide and horizontal if they are wider than they are tall. Don't fight the format. If your painting is in a vertical format, it requires a vertical composition.

Here there are more verticals than just the trees. The reflections in the water are vertical, as is the graduation in the sky. Even the positive and negative spaces create a vertical flow.

Various shapes can be used to draw the eye from one area of a composition to another. One good trick is to use letters of the alphabet. Here the letter U was used to guide the eye down and then up to the subject.

The letter Z was used here. The viewer enters the picture by following the shadows across the grass, up the strong vertical of the tree trunks, then follows the Z shape down and across the picture. The shadow from the rock carries the eye back to the vertical tree trunks.

Repeating or "echoing" shapes is a good way to harmonize composition and create flow. The S shape in the bird's neck was repeated throughout this composition. The flow of the stream bank, the ripples off the water and the branches in the foreground all echo the curve of the bird's neck.

ENLARGING AND TRANSFERRING

*T*here are four different ways to enlarge your designs to their finished size and transfer them. As professionals, we have used all four of these techniques at one time or another, but the one we use most frequently is the overhead projector. The other three methods are using an opaque projector, using a slide projector, or enlarging the pattern using the grid method.

Finished Scale Drawing

We begin by doing small "thumbnail" sketches to work out the composition and values of the mural before making a final drawing. The final drawing is smaller in scale than the final work of art will be, so it must be enlarged. To do this you need to make your finished drawing to the scale that your actual mural will be. First you must measure the area where your mural will go. Many times we will work in what is called a 1-inch scale (1 inch equals 1 foot), (2.5cm equals 30cm) though you can work in any scale such as ¼-inch (6mm), ⅛-inch (3mm), ½-inch (12mm), etc. If you are using 1-inch scale and you have a wall that is 8 feet (2.4m) tall by 12 feet (3.6m) long, you would need to make your final drawing 8 inches by 12 inches (2.4cm by 3.6cm) so that it stays proportionately the same as the wall when you enlarge it. This scale drawing is important in each of the enlarging processes.

Enlarging With a Grid Pattern

To enlarge by the grid technique shown on page 54, you need to overlay a square grid pattern on top of your finished design. Each 1-inch (2.5cm) square, when enlarged to full size, will equal 1 foot (30cm). Sometimes you will want to use a smaller grid, such as ¼-inch (6mm) squares, which would equal 3-inch (7.6cm) squares when enlarged. The size of grid you use depends upon how much detail is in the drawing. The more detail the drawing has, the smaller the grid should be.

Once you have established your grid size, you can draw a grid pattern directly on the wall using something you can easily paint over, such as chalk or light pencil.

Transferring a Cartoon

This is the technique that Michelangelo used to transfer his drawings for the Sistine Chapel. The grid is drawn on large pieces of craft paper or newsprint. Once the grid is drawn, sketch the image inside of each corresponding square from the original finished drawing to the enlarged drawing. The finished enlarged drawing is now called a cartoon.

The next step is to transfer the cartoon onto the wall itself. First the design is perforated with a pounce wheel, which is pictured on page 55. Then tape up each piece of paper on the wall in its appropriate area and use a chalk bag (a piece of cotton rag with powdered chalk in it) and pounce over the perforated holes. The chalk will go through the holes and recreate your pattern underneath. The color of the chalk must contrast with the wall color so you can easily see it, but do not use the red or yellow ground chalk found in hardware stores because it is a permanent chalk. Use the blue or white chalk or baby powder by itself or mixed with the chalk.

Once the cartoon is transferred, the image is easily smeared, so lightly draw over the chalk lines with a pencil. Michelangelo would trace right over his cartoon onto the plaster wall, slightly indenting the wall with his knife to etch the lines into the plaster.

Although these methods are time-consuming, you will need to use grids and cartoons when you do not have enough distance to use a projector or if the light in the room is too bright for a projected image to show up. When conditions are right, using a projector is a quick and easy way to transfer your drawing to the wall. Michelangelo would have been envious.

At this high school, the walls were 30 feet (9m) tall and 300 feet (90m) long. The surface was too large to project the original designs, so we used the grid system, which worked perfectly.

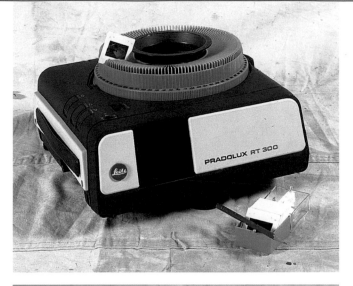

Overhead Projector

The overhead projector is designed to be used with a transparency to enlarge a line drawing by projecting the image onto a vertical surface. You must still make your line drawing to scale for the space you are working on. Once you have drawn your design, you can photocopy it onto a clear transparency.

There are two ways to adjust the size of your image: One is a control knob on the projector and the other is by varying the distance you have the projector from the wall. The farther away from the wall the projector is, the larger your image. If you try to enlarge a very small image to a great size, your lines will become blurred and very thick. To correct this, you need to make adjustments with the projector or start with a larger transparency design.

Sometimes the projector can't be used in certain rooms because there is not enough distance back from the wall to enlarge your design to the required height. If this is the case, then you can project your image up onto sheets of craft paper, working in a space that will give you the required distance, such as your basement or garage. Then you can use the pounce pattern technique to transfer it to your walls.

Using the overhead projector requires a low level of light in the area where you are projecting the image. In the daytime, turn off all the lights and close the curtains or put a sheet over the windows and doors. We sometimes use the overhead just to enlarge certain detail elements in the mural, such as the animals, people or buildings.

Opaque Projectors

Opaque projectors are used like overhead projectors, but they can project directly from a photograph, a magazine clipping, a transparency, or a picture out of a book. This allows you to enlarge a copyright-free design or a personal photograph. Opaque projectors require lower light levels than overhead projectors.

Slide Projector

Like the opaque projector, a slide projector requires a darkened room. The benefit of using a slide projector is that you can use all the wonderful slides you've taken for mural design ideas. Keeping a loaded camera in the car is handy when you come across the perfect clouds, trees, animals, stone wall, buildings or other subject matter for your murals.

Opaque projector (left) and overhead projector (right)

At the same high school as shown on the previous page, we were able to use the overhead projector for the large detailed panels.

Enlarging Your Design

Grid Method

1 › Start your grid enlargement process by drawing a grid pattern over your original design. This grid uses ¼-inch (6mm) squares.

2 › Enlarge your pattern by transferring the line work inside each ¼-inch (6mm) grid block to its corresponding 6-inch (15cm) grid block on the wall. Use chalk because it is easy to erase. Only a portion of the design is shown here. Continue the process for the entire image. Then follow the directions for painting the image.

This is a pounce wheel, which perforates the craft paper so that the lines of your drawing can be transferred to the wall.

Cartoon Method

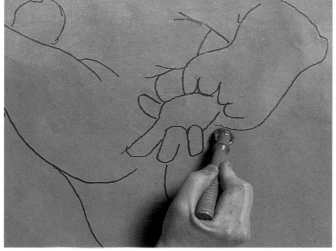

1 › To create the cartoon, project the drawing onto one or more sheets of craft paper and trace over the lines. Use the pounce wheel to perforate the paper on the lines you have drawn. The wheel will make better holes if you first place the craft paper on a soft surface, such as carpet or corrugated cardboard.

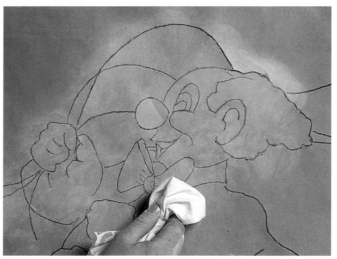

2 › Fill a cloth bag with chalk or baby powder and tie shut. Position your cartoon where you want it, and tape it securely to the wall. Now pat the pounce bag over the perforated holes to transfer the design.

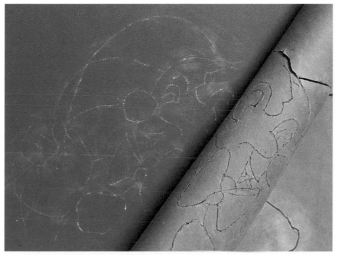

3 › Very carefully remove the cartoon, taking care not to smear the chalk on the wall. The image is fragile at this point, so you will want to trace over it immediately.

4 › Trace over the powder lines with a pencil, colored pencil or stick of chalk. Choose something that you will be able to see, yet that will easily be covered by the paint.

Projects

THIS IS THE PART OF THE BOOK WE ARE SURE YOU WILL FIND THE MOST ENJOYABLE. IT IS IN THESE NEXT PROJECTS THAT WE WILL GUIDE YOU THROUGH THE ART OF MURAL PAINTING. IF YOU FOLLOW THE PROJECTS IN THE ORDER IN WHICH THEY ARE WRITTEN, YOU WILL PROGRESS FROM THE MOST BASIC STYLE OF MURAL PAINTING TO MORE ADVANCED TECHNIQUES. EACH PROJECT HAS ITS OWN BEAUTY AND STYLE AND SHOWS YOU WONDERFUL WAYS TO PAINT A VARIETY OF MURALS. LEARN EACH STYLE SO THAT YOU CAN USE THAT STYLE WITH YOUR OWN DESIGNS. EVENTUALLY YOU WILL BE ABLE TO CREATE YOUR OWN UNIQUE STYLE. THE MURALS FROM THIS BOOK MAY CERTAINLY BE REPRODUCED, BUT WHAT WE REALLY WANT IS FOR YOU TO USE THIS SECTION AS A REFERENCE BOOK AND A TEXTBOOK THAT WILL HELP YOU LEARN TO PAINT MURALS AT MANY DIFFERENT LEVELS OF DIFFICULTY.

ALWAYS PHOTOGRAPH YOUR COMPLETED PROJECTS. IT WON'T TAKE LONG FOR YOU TO HAVE YOUR OWN PORTFOLIO OF MURALS. WE WOULD LOVE TO SEE THE WORK YOU WERE ABLE TO DO WITH THE HELP FROM OUR BOOK. PLEASE SEND ANY PHOTOS YOU WISH TO GARY LORD AND DAVE SCHMIDT, C/O PRISMATIC PAINTING STUDIO, 935 W. GALBRAITH RD., CINCINNATI, OHIO 45231.

Silhouettes

Materials

- design of your own or a copyright-free design
- transparency of design
- overhead projector
- pencil
- 9"-wide (22cm) paint roller and frame
- paint tray
- paint colors of your choice
- AquaCreme
- 2" (51mm) latex sash brush
- ½", ¾", and 1" (12, 19, 25mm) flat brushes
- softening brush to blend colors
- Beugler striping tool
- 4'-long (1.2m) level

One of the nicest and easiest ways to introduce yourself to mural painting is by doing silhouettes. If you can paint inside the line, you can paint silhouettes. Commercial artists, illustrators and muralists frequently turn to this eye-catching technique for its highly decorative quality and its ability to capture a theme subtly. In this chapter you will learn how to design silhouettes, enlarge them to the size you wish and paint them.

Anywhere you think a mural might work, you can consider a silhouette as an option. You can create the silhouettes in any motif: a sports theme for a child's room or recreational room, fitness characters for your exercise room, movie stars for a theater room, animals for a child's room or a landscape mural for a powder room. With these step-by-step instructions and your own creativity, the options are unlimited.

Our pattern for this project came from Elegant Silhouettes of the Twenties, *edited by Bonnie Welch and printed by Dover Publications in 1987. Dover books are inexpensive and they provide great reference material for mural art.*

1 START THE SKY BACKGROUND

For this mural the background will be painted before the silhouette is projected and drawn. This mural was done in a latex low-luster paint applied with a brush. The image should be projected on the wall first to establish placement. Begin the faded evening sky by blocking in the colors starting at the ceiling line, using your darkest blue color. Use two shades of blue and blend them together while they are still wet, creating horizontal cloud shapes as you blend. Then bring the lighter blue downward and create a lavender tone by mixing in a little red and white.

2 CONTINUE WITH THE SKY REFLECTION

Fade the lavender color into an orange yellow toward the horizon line. From the horizon line, reverse the same colors, fading into the darkest blue at the base of the picture. While the paint is wet, add a yellow sun and blend the color down into the water as a reflection. Let this dry. Now go back and do a smoother blend and make the colors more opaque by first applying AquaCreme, which acts as a retarder and blending agent. Then follow the same steps as above to make the colors more opaque.

3 REFINE THE SKY

Keep blending the colors, working from top to bottom until you are satisfied. You'll notice that the AquaCreme makes the paint easier to blend.

4 TRACE SILHOUETTE ON BACKGROUND

Once the background dries, project the silhouette image onto it and trace the outline. You may also use any of the other transfer techniques discussed on pages 52 to 55.

5 FILL IN THE SILHOUETTE

To paint the silhouettes themselves, use a 2-inch (51mm) latex sash brush to define the larger contour shapes and a small flat artist's brush to paint the more detailed contour shapes. Because of the scale of this piece, most of the work was done with artist's brushes. On larger work, once the silhouette is outlined, you can use either a 3-inch, 7-inch or 9-inch (7.6, 17.8, or 22cm) roller handle and paint sleeve to roll the remaining areas with the latex paint. If the silhouette color doesn't cover in one coat, apply a second coat. We intentionally made the outside border of this silhouette irregular. You will see from the pictures of other silhouettes that sometimes there are no borders at all.

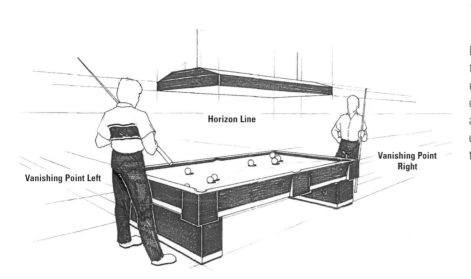

Horizon Line

Vanishing Point Right

Vanishing Point Left

1 PROJECT DRAWING ON WALL

This project shows red colored pencil lines indicating the perspective lines used in the drawing, which is in blue pencil. You can use an overhead projector to enlarge your drawing up to wall size. You need to be sure all of your perspective lines "click" before enlarging. A small error will be magnified tremendously when the drawing is enlarged.

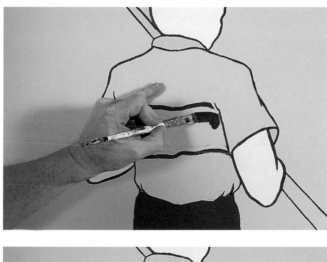

2 OUTLINE THE IMAGE

When you are painting over the extisting wall color, all you need to do is select a color that harmonizes with the colors in the room and paint inside the lines you have drawn. An artist's brush is handy for outlining solid areas before filling them in with a larger brush.

3 FILL IN THE SOLID AREAS

Save time by filling in the larger areas with a wider brush. See the next page for tips on making perfectly straight lines using a Beugler striping tool.

Using a Beugler Striping Tool

The Beugler striping tool comes with various size heads for different size stripes.

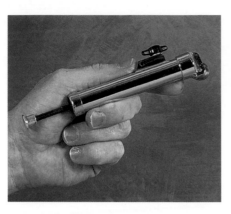

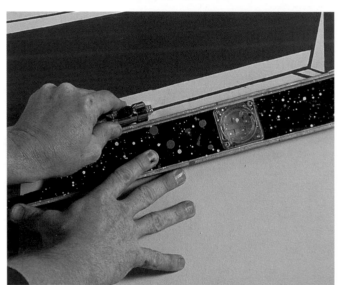

Use this tool instead of a liner brush when you want to create straight, even lines.

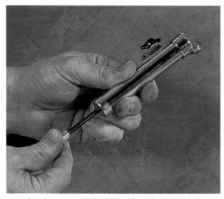

1 › Do not thin your paint. Thinned paint can cause your lines to bleed.

2 › Apply the striping head and slightly depress the plunger until a small amount of paint saturates the wheel.

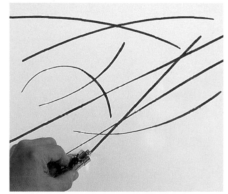

3 › Use the striping tool by pulling it toward you with a firm, even pressure. Various size lines can be executed with the same head depending on the angle at which you hold the head to the wall.

TOP *Painting an interesting background behind your silhouette is a simple way to add drama and impact.*

BOTTOM *Note how the black lion, column, and Statue of Liberty appear to come forward; that's because dark colors advance and light colors recede. Also note how multiple colors on the bridge and stonework add extra dimension. Use of positive and negative space also creates a feeling of dimension and interest.*

2-D Graphic & Shaded Murals

Materials

- design of your own or a copyright-free design
- pencil
- chalk
- pounce bag
- paint colors of your choice (we used blue-violet, yellow-orange, red, green, orange, blue, white and black)
- AquaCreme
- two rulers, 12" and 3' (30cm and 1m) for enlarging by the grid method
- various art brushes
- craft paper
- pounce wheel
- clear polyurethane

In this chapter you will go to the next level of mural painting by adding a more dimensional aspect to your work. This will be accomplished by using a line drawing with multiple colors. By juxtaposing different color values and hues, you will achieve a sense of depth.

This clown can be left as solid colored shapes, which we call a 2-D graphic mural. This type of mural is especially suitable for a child's wall. You can also go one step further by adding shading and highlights to give the image a more substantial and solid appearance. The final step is to outline the shapes, which really makes the image seem to pop right off of the wall surface. We call this a 2-D shaded mural. By following the steps in creating the clown mural, you will see for yourself how each step helps create the finished dimensional effect. Then you can get inspiration from our gallery of 2-D graphic and 2-D shaded murals.

See pages 54 and 55 for information on enlarging this image using the grid and cartoon methods. However, if you have an opaque projector, you could simply project the image of the finished clown mural from this book and trace the outlines directly on your wall.

1 BEGIN PAINTING

For graphic painting you can just butt up color to color using a brush or roller. You can see in this color scheme the use of complementary (blue-violet background and yellow-orange stars; red and green; orange and blue) and analogous colors (blue and blue-violet; orange and yellow-orange). If you have a Beugler striping tool, use it for the balloon strings.

2 FILL IN ALL THE COLOR AREAS

Notice how the background color is left to define where the clown's legs and arms have folds in the fabric. You will probably need to paint two or more coats to completely cover the background color. The paints were used without thinning to achieve a nice, opaque appearance. You may like the look of the mural at this point and want to leave it as a 2-D graphic mural. That is one choice you can make.

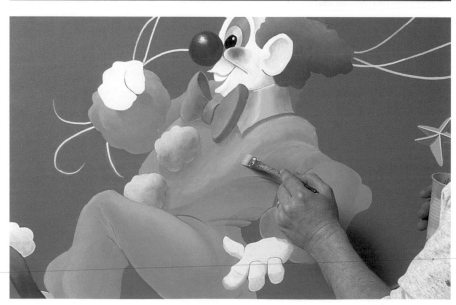

3 ADD HIGHLIGHTS

If you want to take your mural one step further, add highlights, shading and outlines. First, be sure that the paint is completely dry. The highlights go on first. The light source is from the top right, so put the highlights on top of the hair, shoulder, knees, shoes and tops of the balloons. In the areas you are going to highlight, paint an undercoat of AquaCreme the way you did for the silhouette sky; only this time, when you paint in your highlight color, blend it out with a dry brush into the dry base color. This gives nice, soft transitions in your highlight areas.

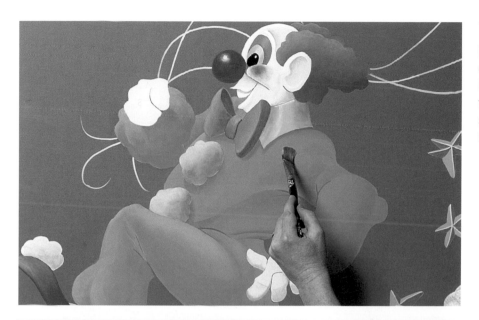

4 ADD SHADING

Add shading to the bottom of the balloons, legs, arms and feet the same way you did the highlights. Use AquaCreme and blend out the shading color for a smooth transition. Notice that the shadows on the stars are created with orange and the highlights are white lines.

5 COMPLETE THE HIGHLIGHTS AND SHADING

Use this photo as a reference for your highlights and shadows. Compare this to the flat graphic style in step 2, and you will see the extra dimension added to the work. The next step will make the image "pop."

6 ADD BLACK OUTLINES

Use a liner brush to add outlines. Note that the paint can is securely taped to the top of the ladder. This will help avoid a catastrophe!

7 SEAL THE MURAL

If you want the surface to be protected for extra durability, coat it with clear polyurethane after the paint is thoroughly dry. The best way is to spray this on using a spray gun (spray polyurethane works too, but it will take several cans). You can also use a brush or roller.

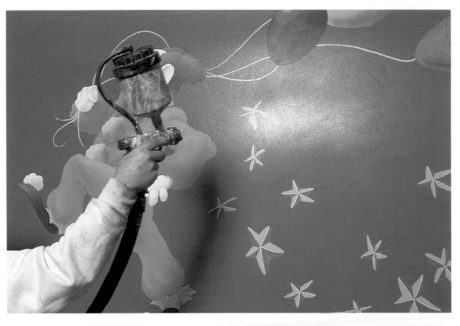

Now step back and admire your work. Although the clown would have been acceptable with flat colors, you can see how adding the extras contributes to its appearance.

The addition of shading creates the illusion that this boy's room is really a space station.

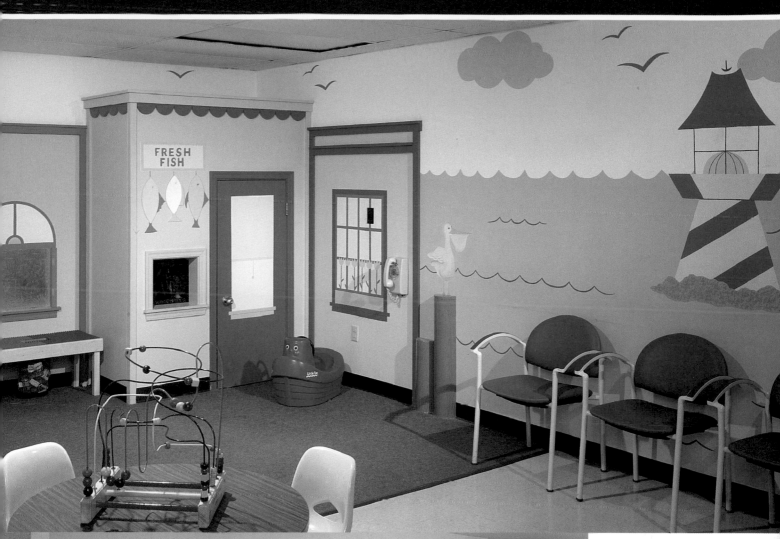

Designs From Wallpaper & Fabric

Materials

- design of your own choice
- tracing paper
- pencil
- chalk line
- blue masking tape
- paint colors to go with your pattern
- tape measure
- various artist's brushes
- transfer paper or graphite paper

A muralist can pick and choose from design elements that are already in a home to accent other areas just as a music arranger rearranges a composer's score to fit his needs or a chef combines ingredients in a unique way for a marvelous new taste. In this chapter you will learn how to pick out design elements from fabrics, carpet, draperies, wallpaper or furniture and adapt them to your wall decorating needs. You can either copy a part of a design element and repeat it on the walls, or you can use a design as a foundation and embellish it.

When selecting a design, you must consider the area you are decorating. Look at the other elements in the room, such as furniture, cabinets, floor treatment and curtains. For example, you may have a new kitchen with nice cabinets, a contemporary hardwood floor and window treatments, but the walls seem plain. You could pull a border design from the curtain fabric and use it in accent areas above the sink, doorways, stove and around windows. Although you may not want to duplicate this project exactly, you can see how to use this process to fit your own individual needs.

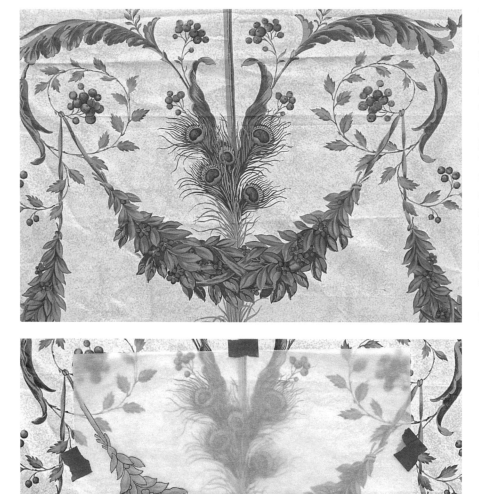

1 CHOOSE YOUR DESIGN

A copy machine can be used to enlarge or reduce a pattern. If you are doing a continuous border, you will need to measure the wall and create the design so it divides evenly in the given space. For example, if the wall is 12 feet (3.6m) long, you could make each design 12 inches (30cm) long and repeat it twelve times. If you want the design to be a certain size, but it won't fit evenly in the given space, a space between the designs will make up for the odd measurements. For example, if you have 155 inches (393.7cm) of wall space and the design is 12 inches (30cm) long, you could put eleven spaces between the twelve designs with each space measuring 1 inch (2.5cm).

In this example, the design is taken from fabric.

2 TRACE THE DESIGN

Use tracing paper and trace the design from the fabric.

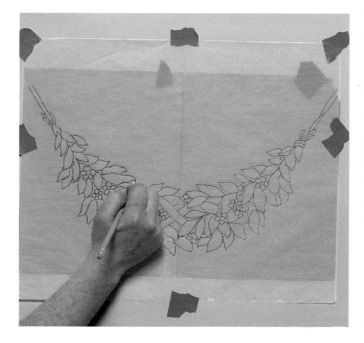

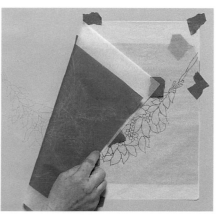

3 TRANSFER THE DESIGN TO THE WALL

Use transfer paper or graphite paper to transfer the design to the area you wish to work on. If you use a piece of transfer paper that is close to the paint color, it will be easier to hide the lines when painting. When transferring a design, you need to have a registration line to ensure that your pattern stays in correct alignment. You can make a registration mark by snapping a level chalk line to connect with the top of the design so that it will stay consistent and level.

4 BLOCK IN THE COLORS

To paint the swag in this design, match the paint colors to those in the fabric as closely as possible. Start out by blocking in the solid colors of the leaves and berries, alternating the lights and darks next to each other.

5 SHADE AND HIGHLIGHT
In areas based in a light color, add dark accents; add light accents for areas based in a dark color.

6 ADD DETAILS
Use a little liner brush to add the small details.

Now connect as many swags as you wish to create your design around the room.

OPPOSITE PAGE › *The main rose floral element from the draperies was repeated to accent this corner cabinet.*

TOP › *The design from the wallpaper border was extended to the wall itself in this playful, yet pretty girl's room.*

BOTTOM › *This kitchen border was adapted from the curtains.*

Using Stencils

Materials

- AquaBond Off White latex paint in Yellow Ochre
- Delta Creamcoat paint: English Yew, Boston Fern, Burnt Umber, Misty Mauve, Rose Mist, Raw Sienna, Palomino Tan, Spice Tan, and Sonoma Wine
- AquaGlaze
- stencil (We used Dee-Signs, Ltd. #502 Aubusson)
- 3 stencil brushes of each of the following sizes: ½" (12mm); ¾" (19mm) ; ¼" (6mm)
- 4" (10cm) paint brush
- coarse steel wool
- spray adhesive
- tape measure
- level for making vertical lines

You can paint either part of or an entire mural using ready-made stencils from today's wonderful stencil designers and manufacturers. Using stencils for a repetitive pattern is more efficient than tracing a design over and over. The room shown on this and the previous page was stenciled in less than one day (although it took part of the previous day to glaze the walls before stenciling). Stencils can be used with other techniques as a time-saver. If you want to paint a border of flowers and leaves, you can cut stencils for the basic leaf and flower shapes, use highlighting and shading to give the shapes more dimension, then paint the stems and vines.

If you are using a design in multiple applications around the room, stencil that design everywhere it belongs before moving on to the next stencil. This is a faster, more organized way to approach the project. When stenciling, use only a little bit of paint on the tip of your stencil brush and remove any excess paint on a paper towel before painting inside the stencil. You can either pounce or swirl the brush to transfer the paint to the wall.

The repetition of this stenciled design around the room gives the room a feeling of harmony.

1 BASECOAT THE WALL

Basecoat the wall in AquaBond Off White, then let it dry.

2 GLAZE THE WALL

Mix a glaze of four parts AquaGlaze and one part Yellow Ochre latex paint. Working in a 2'- to 3'-wide (60.9 to 91cm) strip from ceiling to floor, brush glaze on the wall. Paint a light coat with a 4-inch (10cm) brush in a vertical pattern. The trick is to be sure you have enough glaze on so that it stays wet while you are working, but not so much that you will spend a lot of time removing the excess.

3 REMOVE THE EXCESS GLAZE

While the glaze is still wet, drag a piece of coarse steel wool vertically through it several times to get the desired effect. Repeat the process of step 2 and step 3 until you have glazed all of the walls. Let dry 24 hours.

4 POSITION THE LEFT OVERLAY

Determine the placement for the design. This design is centered inside the panels, starting 3 inches (7.6cm) down from the top. The center of each panel is marked in chalk with a vertical line, which is used to line up each stencil.

5 STENCIL THE FIRST COLOR

Select the colors and have one brush for each color you are using. Spray adhesive on the back of the stencils to help them adhere to the wall. This stencil consists of eight individual parts called overlays, four for the left side, and four for the right. Although they are numbered by the manufacturer, it is wise to number them in marker LF1 for the first left front side, LF2 for the second one, and so forth. Also highlight the center vertical line on all the overlays so you won't have any trouble identifying which one goes on which side.

6 STENCIL THE OTHER COLORS

Be sure paint does not get underneath the edge of the overlay. Smudges will be difficult to repair because of the glazing. Pounce or swirl the colors in the stencil, using a separate brush for each color.

7 COMPLETED LEFT SIDE

Carefully lift off the overlay to avoid smudging the wet paint. Now the first overlay, LF1, is finished.

8 USE FIRST OVERLAY ON RIGHT SIDE

Line up the right side the same way you did the left. This will be the overlay marked RF1. Stencil in the colors for this overlay.

This shows the design after the first two overlays have been completed.

9 USE SECOND OVERLAY, LEFT SIDE AND RIGHT SIDE

Stencil in all colors one at a time. When LF2 is complete, stencil the colors for RF2.

The second overlay on the left side is completed.

This shows overlay RF2 being stenciled.

10 USE THE THIRD OVERLAYS

This will be the overlay marked LF3. Stencil the colors one at a time, as you did before. Then position RF3 and stencil those colors.

This shows the design after the third overlay left side has been painted.

This shows the design after the third overlays have been completed.

11 USE THE FOURTH OVERLAYS

This will be the overlay marked LF4.
Stencil the colors, and remove the overlay.
Position RF4 and stencil those colors.

This shows the design after completion of the fourth overlay left side.

This shows stenciling overlay RF4.

This shows the completed design.

OPPOSITE PAGE › *The leaves were stencils, and the trees were drawn and painted.*
TOP › *The leaves and grapes were stencils, and the vines were handpainted.*
BOTTOM LEFT › *The flower pattern in this painted stair runner was stenciled.*
BOTTOM RIGHT › *This wall and ceiling shows a combination of stencils and handwork.*

Painting Skies & Clouds

Materials for Brushing Clouds

- plant mister spray bottle
- sea sponge
- 2" (5cm) chip brush
- 3" (7.6cm) sash brush
- 4" (10cm) sash brush
- paint roller
- 4" (10cm) foam roller
- paint tray
- Benjamin Moore latex satin paints (sold by number, not by name) 769, 788, 890, 804

Materials for Spraying Clouds

- airbrush or automobile touch-up gun
- compressor
- Benjamin Moore latex satin paints: 038, 370, 769, 890

What better way to add subtle warmth and openness to a room than with a beautiful sky mural? On walls or ceilings, in dining rooms, nurseries or studies, sky murals can add life and a sense of movement to a room. Skies don't have to be just a large blue mass with white fluffy clouds. To create drama in your sky, a storm cloud can be added to the corner of the mural. This is also a great way to add movement to your sky, as the viewer wonders if the storm is moving in or out. For more interest, consider adding birds, butterflies or a few fall leaves.

Clouds can be sprayed, ragged, sponged, brushed or a combination of all four. Spraying clouds with an airbrush or touch-up gun is fast and a great way to achieve soft, subtle effects. Check tool rental shops for compressors and spray equipment if spraying your sky mural is the direction you want to go. The results can be well worth the effort.

Before starting, keep in mind that if you paint your clouds on the ceiling, the viewing point is different from those on walls. Look overhead at the clouds on a nice day. You are seeing mainly the bottom of the clouds, the shaded area. Now look out toward the horizon and notice that the stronger highlights are seen on top because of the viewing angle.

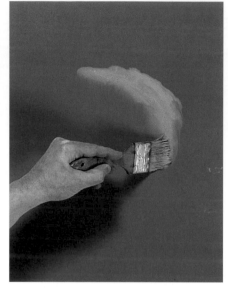

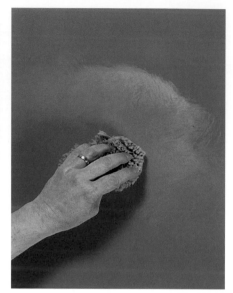

1 BASECOAT THE WALL
Paint your wall in the sky color, Benjamin Moore 769, and let dry. Use a spray bottle to mist the area where you want to place your first cloud. Roll over the water with a 4-inch (10cm) foam roller to even it out. The water will slow down the drying time of the latex paint, giving you more time to work with it.

2 LAY IN THE CLOUDS
Using your 2-inch (6cm) brush, form the outside edge of your cloud with the cloud base color, Benjamin Moore 788 latex satin.

3 SPONGE THE CLOUDS
While the paint is still wet, soften the color toward the inside of the cloud with a damp sea sponge.

4 BUILD UP LAYERS OF WHITE
Build your edges up in layers like rolling hills to add dimension to the clouds. After this has dried, step back and look at the clouds and decide where you want to beef up the shapes. This will be done by repeating the first step. As you apply the same color again in select areas, the color will become more opaque, giving the cloud a fuller, denser look, while leaving the other areas with a lighter, airy look.

5 DECIDE WHERE THE LIGHTEST AREAS WILL BE

As you are doing this, keep in mind where your imaginary light source (the sun) is. The edge of thc clouds facing the light source is where the strongest highlight will be placed.

6 HIGHLIGHT

Add highlights in Benjamin Moore 890 using your sash brush. Thin your color slightly with water and stipple the highlight on. (Remember your light source.)

7 REMOVE EXTRA PAINT
Knock off the excess paint on a piece of board or paper.

8 BLEND
Blend the highlight areas with the same brush in a circular motion toward the center of the cloud.

9 ADD SHADOWS

To create greater dimension within the clouds, add shadows. The first shadow color will be the same color we used for the blue sky, Benjamin Moore 769. When you built your clouds up by layering the edges, you created hills and valleys. The valleys are the areas for the shadows. Dilute your color to turn it into a transparent wash, brush it into the valleys and fade it out toward the highlighted area of the cloud. Be careful not to cover the highlighted ridge of the cloud in front of the shadow. The color can also be used to push back any areas you feel are too strong. After diluting it further, brush over those areas and soften with a damp sponge. A second shadow color, Benjamin Moore 804, can be added to each cloud on top of the first in areas furthest from your light source. Now step back to see if any additional highlights or shadows are needed.

The finished brushed sky.

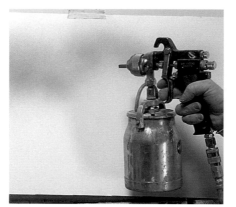

2 TEST THE SPRAY

Have a piece of cardboard handy to test your spray. This paint is too thick. If it appears grainy and it is hard to spray, the paint is too thick.

If the paint is too thin, it will be runny and will bead on the wall. Keep the spray gun at a 90° angle to the wall, about 6 to 12 inches (15 to 30cm) away.

1 PREPARE THE PAINT

This time, instead of adding white clouds to a blue background, blue will be sprayed onto a cloud-colored background. Apply the base color with a paint roller and allow to dry. This wall was painted with Benjamin Moore 890 latex paint. Use a flat latex paint for a ceiling, but use a satin or eggshell base for walls so they can be cleaned if soiled. A cup gun was used for this demonstration. Thin some Benjamin Moore 769 with water to the consistency of light cream and strain the paint through a nylon panty hose to remove any lumps. Fill the spray cup about three-quarters full and fasten it to the gun. Make sure it is securely fastened! For this gun, set the pressure between 30 and 40 psi.

3 BEGIN SPRAYING THE SKY

The first color is the sky color, Benjamin Moore 769. Pull the trigger about halfway and lightly spray to establish the size, shape and location of your clouds. Make the first pass very light so corrections will be simple. Large blue sky areas can quickly be filled in by pulling back on the trigger all the way. To prevent runs and buildup, start moving the gun before you pull the trigger, and release the trigger before you stop.

4 STOP AND STEP BACK

Now that your clouds are roughed in, step back and see if you are satisfied with the overall composition. If so, shape your clouds with the same sky blue color and fill in any thin areas. Depending on the look you are going for, this could be a completed sky. Note that diagonal drifts to your sky work better than horizontal or vertical.

5 FURTHER DEFINE THE CLOUDS

To add further shape and definition to your clouds, shade with Benjamin Moore 038 flat latex paint.

6 ADD HIGHLIGHTS

Highlight the areas closest to your imaginary light source with Benjamin Moore 370. To finish the mural, load the gun with the base color, Benjamin Moore 890, and lightly mist over the clouds and into the blue. This will soften the clouds and the sky together. Hold the gun back farther from the surface to mist the area.

The completed sprayed sky.

This night sky was painted with a cup gun and airbrush. The sky accurately depicts the stars in the Northern hemisphere at the Summer Solstice.

OPPOSITE PAGE › *This sky was sprayed with a cup gun and airbrush.*

TOP › *The wall behind the bed does have a recessed alcove, but the windows on either side of it are painted, as are the stones.*

BOTTOM › *This very dramatic sky shows that clouds don't have to be just white, fluffy masses on a blue background.*

Creating Realistic Textures

Materials

- Benjamin Moore latex paint: 105, 232, 242, 433, 441, 518, 525, 546, 700, 1225, 1531, 1538, 1552, 1577, 1595, 1601, HC-70
- AquaColor in Earth Green and Earth Brown
- latex paint in black and red
- AquaCreme
- 3" (7.6cm) and regular size paint roller
- various artist's brushes
- chalk
- level and straightedges
- blue masking tape
- spray bottle

Project Six

The earth tones and varied textures in this project are relaxing and pleasing. This mural adds a certain richness to a room, and it would be a great backdrop for the aged Southwestern furniture that is so popular today.

The variety of textures makes this rather simple composition interesting. The soft, rounded edges of the stones and subtle shading create a very calming effect. It's easy to "get lost" in the nooks and crannies between the stones. The aged, weather-beaten wooden door adds contrast with its strong horizontal and vertical lines and textured woodgrain, yet its gentle curving lines echo the shapes of the stones.

The vine adds to the composition by creating a stronger sense of depth The vine casts shadows onto the wall, giving the feeling that it's closer to the viewer. The tangled branches of the vine repeat the shapes of the dark areas between the stones. The green of the vine is complementary to the reddish color of the stones, and the vine is essential for breaking up the hard edge of the header above the door.

The textures in this mural were a great deal of fun to paint, and this project pulls together everything you have learned in this book. We hope you enjoy painting this as much as we did.

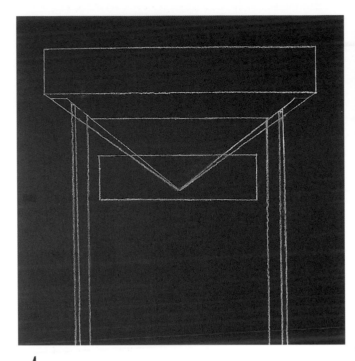

1 BASECOAT THE WALL

Paint the wall with black paint that has a touch of red to make the color richer. After the paint dries, draw the door using one-point perspective and a level. Since the stone wall will be painted first, use blue tape to tape off the inside edges of the door, including the door frame and header. (See step 11 for a photo of this.)

2 ADD FIRST SCUMBLE

Next, add the first of three scumbles to the rock area. With a 3-inch (7.6cm) roller, roll on a coat of B.M. 700 in a small patch about the size of a dinner plate. Immediately soften the edge with a soft, damp cotton rag. Then move on to the area next to it, roll on the paint, then soften with a rag. Continue until the entire rock area is scumbled.

3 ADD SECOND SCUMBLE

Add another scumble over the first one. Roll on a coat of B.M. 1538 about the size of a dinner plate, then soften with a rag. If you try to do more than a dinner plate-size area at one time, the paint will dry too quickly and you won't be able to soften it. Continue until the entire rock area is scumbled.

4 ADD THIRD SCUMBLE

Roll on a coat of B.M. 1531 and repeat the scumbling process. The three scumbles combined will be the background for the stone blocks.

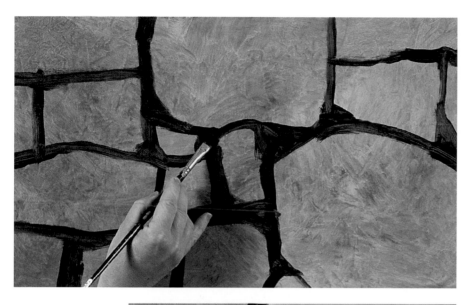

5 BEGIN DEFINING ROCKS

Draw in the stones with chalk. Then use the same black paint you used for the basecoat to paint the shadow areas between the stones with a ¾- or ½-inch (19 or 12mm) brush. Notice how the line varies from thick to thin.

6 HIGHLIGHT STONES

Thin B.M. 242 with water to make a wash and use a 2-inch (5cm) chip brush in a scrubbing motion to highlight each stone. The top and right sides of the stones will be highlighted.

7 PUT FIRST WASH ON STONES

Thin B.M. 105 to make a wash, then lightly spray the stone area with water. Roll over the surface with a clean paint roller to break up the water droplets. While the surface is still wet, apply the wash with a brush. Using a synthetic sponge, blot the area to remove excess paint and brushstrokes. Your highlights should still show through. Let dry.

8 APPLY THE SECOND WASH

Apply B.M. HC-70 the same way as in step 7, using the water bottle to spray the wall first. The only difference is that you will only apply the wash to the lower left areas of the stones.

9 BLOT THE WASH

Before the wash dries, blot and blend it with the sponge.

10 SPATTER THE STONES

Spatter the stones with the black paint, then with one of the scumble colors. Thin the paint with water to get smaller spatter. Use a 2-inch (5cm) chip brush for a spatter tool.

11 TAPE AND PAINT THE DOOR

Next, tape off every other plank of the door. Thin B.M. 1595 slightly with water. Using a 2-inch (5cm) chip brush, apply color in one continuous stroke from top to bottom. Use very little pressure. This is how the woodgrain pattern is established. Use the final photograph to see where to add waves in the grain.

12 ADD MORE WOODGRAIN

The second woodgrain color is B.M. 1225 thinned with water and applied as in the previous step.

13 APPLY THIRD WOOD COLOR

Thin B.M. 441 and repeat the woodgrain process as above. It is not important to cover the whole area. Skip some areas to add interest.

14 HIGHLIGHT THE WOOD

Use B.M. 232 as a highlight color on the wood. This should be applied randomly. Be careful not to overdo this step. After the paint dries, remove the tape and tape off the planks you just painted. Start with step 11 and paint the remaining planks the same way.

15 CREATE CRACKS

When all the planks are woodgrained, use a liner brush to paint the cracks between the planks. Also paint small holes and splits in the wood. Be sure to follow the direction of the grain.

16 STAIN THE WOOD

Mix AquaColor Earth Green, Earth Brown and AquaCreme. Use this slow-drying mix to create a dirty stain for the door. Paint one plank at a time, then wipe off the glaze with cheesecloth, following the direction of the grain. Leave some areas of glaze a little heavier than others to create interesting light and dark values.

17 HIGHLIGHT THE CRACKS

After the wash has dried, use B.M. 232 to highlight the cracks in the planks and the gaps between them. Since the light is coming from the upper right, the highlights will fall on the left side of the black cracks and gaps in the door. Use the black base color to pump up any dark area that may have been lost when the wash was applied.

18 ADD SHADOWS

Use the dirty stain color from step 16 and a ¾-inch (19mm) brush to add shadows to the door, such as shown here. Soften the shadow with a dry chip brush to remove brushstrokes. Nail heads can be created by dipping a pencil eraser in black paint.

19 BEGIN LAYING IN THE VINE

Draw the vine with chalk. Use the black base color to paint the vines with a ¾- or 1-inch (19 or 25mm) brush.

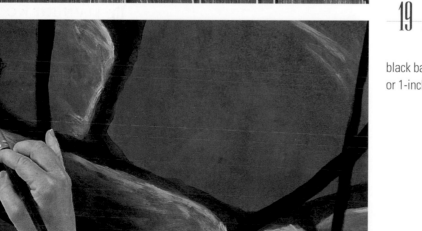

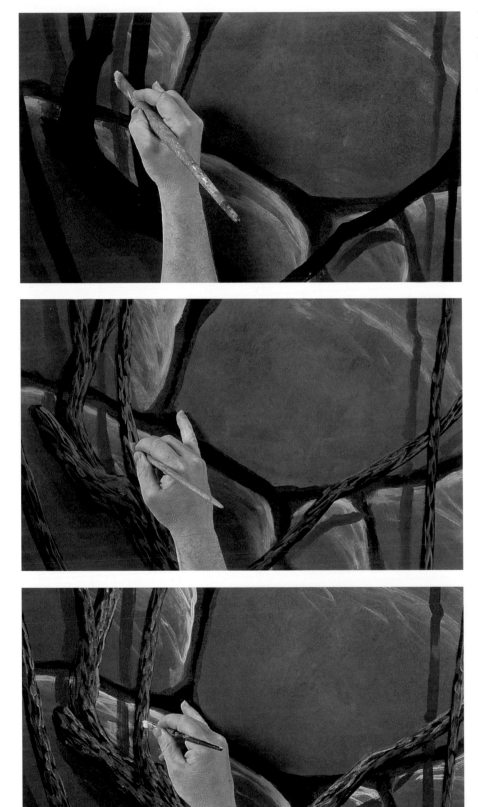

20 PAINT THE SHADOW

After the base color has dried, paint the shadow cast on the wall by the vine using a touch of black and B.M. HC-70. Use a ¾- or 1-inch (19 or 25mm) brush, and keep in mind where your light source is.

21 APPLY FIRST VINE HIGHLIGHTS

The highlights for the vine will be added in three stages. Use B.M. 1601 to lay in the texture of the bark. Use a side-to-side motion with the flat side of the brush, allowing it to bounce on and off the surface. This will give you a series of short, random dashes of color. Follow the direction and contour of the vine when applying the color.

22 APPLY SECOND VINE HIGHLIGHTS

Apply the next color, B.M. 1552 in the same way, only this time start on the highlighted edge of the vine and work the color only three-quarters of the way around the vine. Slowly taper off the color as you approach that point.

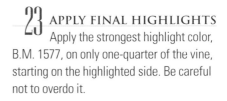

23 APPLY FINAL HIGHLIGHTS
Apply the strongest highlight color, B.M. 1577, on only one-quarter of the vine, starting on the highlighted side. Be careful not to overdo it.

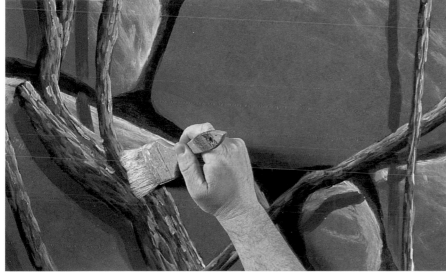

24 ADD A WASH
Now you may add a wash of B.M. 525 to any areas of the vine that you feel are too strong. Selected areas can be wiped with cheesecloth to bring out some of the highlights.

25 LAY IN THE LEAF CLUSTERS
Sketch in the leaf clusters with chalk. Start with the shadow color from step 20 and paint in the areas that will be shadows cast by the leaves. Then paint the leaves with black and purple in a quick one-step stroke. Start with the ¾-inch (19mm) brush vertical to the wall, then pull it along its narrow edge while slowly twisting the brush. This makes a line that starts thin and slowly widens. Then reverse the twist, slowly bringing the brush back to a narrow point. Place your leaves according to the shadows you painted first.

26 ADD GREEN LEAF COLOR

Next, lay in B.M. 518. This needs to be painted with more care. Paint the leaves in clusters of three, and let these clusters overlap each other.

27 ADD FIRST HIGHLIGHTS

The next leaf color is B.M. 546, and it should be painted keeping the light source in mind. Begin to work from the highlighted edge toward the shadowed side of the entire leaf cluster. Carry the color about three-quarters of the way across each leaf.

28 ADD SECOND HIGHLIGHTS

Apply B.M. 433 next, working from the highlight edge and carrying the color over only about halfway across each leaf.

29 **ADD FINAL HIGHLIGHTS**
Finally, use B.M. 430 sparingly for sparkle.

Now the mural is complete!

TOP LEFT › *A butler's pantry door was painted with dishes, tiles, cups and a shelf; the cabinet doors and drawer fronts are real and are mounted over the painted door.*

TOP MIDDLE › *The use of shadows enhances the realistic effect of this delightfully playful mural.*

TOP RIGHT › *A good reference photograph was essential in recreating this moonscape.*

BOTTOM LEFT › *The floor is painted masonite; stucco was added to the walls and shaded; the shutters, thatched roof and door are real.*

BOTTOM MIDDLE › *The lighting and use of shadows make this mural appear 3-D.*

BOTTOM RIGHT › *A real sign is "hung" with a painted wire to the painted tree. Adding a real birdhouse further develops the play between what is 3-D and what is painted illusion.*

The paint used in this mural was latex interior house paint, and the colors were mixed on-site using universal tints. These colorants are similar to what is used in paint stores to tint paint. The tints are extremely concentrated, and it takes very little to make a color by mixing it with white or another color. You can't use tints directly from the bottle; they must be mixed with paint.

Mountain Mural

Materials

- ❖ 2" (5cm) chip brush
- ❖ 1", ¾", ½", ¼" (25, 19, 12, 6mm) flat brushes
- ❖ chalk line
- ❖ paint tray
- ❖ paint roller
- ❖ charcoal pencil or chalk
- ❖ rags
- ❖ plastic cups
- ❖ blue masking tape
- ❖ cup gun and air compressor
- ❖ sea sponge
- ❖ dropcloths

The project detailed in this section was for a client who enjoyed the wide open spaces of the American West. The area for the mural was an eight-sided tray ceiling approximately 15 feet (4.5m) from the floor, 17 feet (5.1m) long and 15 feet (4.5m) wide. The mural was a complete wraparound panoramic mountain scene with the sky trailing across the ceiling. After a drawing of the scene was made, it was transferred to the wall. With a large project such as this, it is essential to make a full-color mock-up to work out any problems beforehand.

Remember, a small dot of color on a mock-up can represent an entire boulder or side of a building when it is enlarged to the size of your wall. Be aware of these things when painting your mock-up.

1 BASECOAT THE WALL

The techniques on pages 102 to 104 can be used here for painting the sky and clouds. Roll on the sky blue color first. Then mix a slightly darker shade by adding purple and spray lightly in random areas to add depth to the sky. Make sure the two colors melt together. Refer to your clip file or photos of mountains to get an idea of the correct size for the clouds in relation to the mountain. Once the sky is dry, you can lay your clouds in.

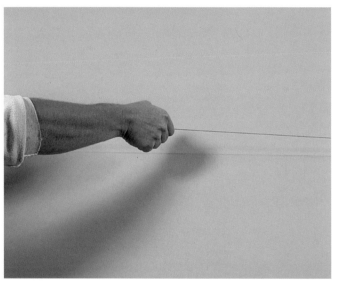

2 SNAP THE HORIZON LINE

Remember that when painting a wall mural—whether it's an architectural scene or landscape—you need to start with a horizon line. This should be at eye level to the viewer, between 5 and 6 feet (1.5 and 1.8m) from the floor. This line can be snapped in using a chalk line.

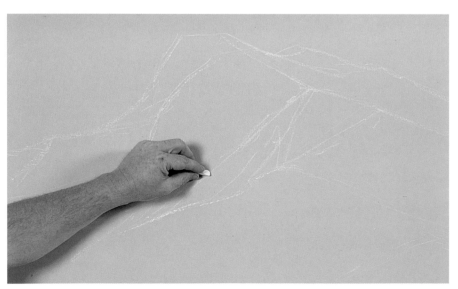

3 TRANSFER THE DESIGN TO THE WALL

Lightly draw your pattern using a charcoal pencil or chalk. An overhead projector can also be used. Mix your first colors in plastic cups and label each color according to what it will be used for (mountain highlights, grass, etc.). You may very well end up with twenty to forty cups of paint by the time your mural is finished.

4 PAINT DISTANT MOUNTAINS

To create distant mountains, you must keep details to a minimum. The colors should be lighter, softer and cooler.

5 SPRAY MOUNTAIN

When the mountain is finished, lightly spray over it with the spray gun, using the same color as the sky. This gives the mountain a realistic sense of atmospheric perspective.

6 KEEP COLORS LIGHT

Don't worry that the mountains seem unfinished and pale; these mountains will look just right when the darker and richer colors are applied later to the foreground.

7 OUTLINE THE MOUNTAIN

Mix dark blue, red and raw umber to create a dark purple. Use this color and loose, free-flowing strokes with the edge of a 2-inch (51mm) brush to lay in the basic lines of your mountain. Allow to dry.

8 ADD A THIN WASH OF COLOR

Dilute some of the color from step 1 with an equal amount of water. This mixture is known as a wash and will be transparent when applied. Cover the entire mountain with this wash using a scrubbing motion and the flat side of a 2-inch (51mm) flat brush. Blot with a rag or damp sea sponge to remove excess color.

9 CHECK YOUR WORK

When dry, the lines brushed on in step 7 should still be visible.

10 APPLY FIRST HIGHLIGHTS

Mix raw umber, yellow ochre and white to make your first highlight color. You will be building up your highlights slowly with each step, so this color should have a slightly lighter value than the base color used in your mountain. Thinning the colors a little with water will help them to flow. With the edge of your ½-inch (12mm) flat brush, follow the contour of your mountain and lay in highlights. Remember to use the same imaginary light source you used for your clouds.

11 STEP BACK AND LOOK

It is very important to stand back from your work as you are painting. This helps you to see how the mural is progressing and prevents you from overworking any one area with details that will not be visible from the normal viewing distance. With your first highlight complete, your mountain should be taking shape.

12 APPLY SECOND HIGHLIGHTS

Add more yellow ochre and white to your first highlight color. Highlight the areas that will receive full sun from your imaginary light source. Begin by highlighting the areas where you're sure light will hit, then stand back to see if you've missed anything. Do not cover your first highlight 100 percent; instead it should be 75 percent coverage, then 25 percent on your next highlight. Allowing each highlight color to show next to the preceding color will create a fade from dark to light.

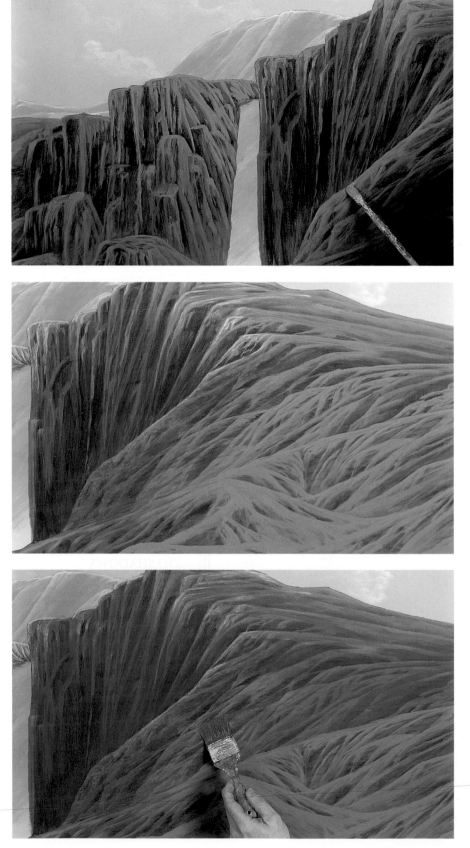

13 APPLY THIRD HIGHLIGHTS

Add red and a little white to the second highlight color to make a slightly more orange color. Mix this in a separate cup using part of your second highlight color in case you need more of your second highlight color later. Apply it along the ridges of your mountain.

14 APPLY FINAL HIGHLIGHT

Adding a light color brings out points of interest and, when applied against a dark background, helps pull the ridge closer to the viewer, creating depth. Notice the much lighter highlights on the tops of the ridges. White was added to the previous color to make this highlight.

15 CREATE DISTANCE

At this point, it is time to create some distance between the mountain and the viewer. With the same wash used in step 8 and a 2-inch (51mm) flat brush, scrub in color following the contour of the mountain. Work quickly and cover about 75 percent of the mountain, letting some true color show through. Add water if your wash is too opaque.

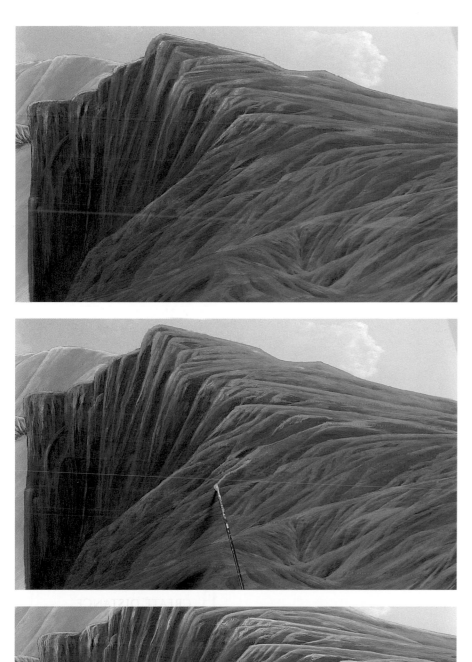

16 CHECK YOUR WORK

Stop! Stand back and study your mountain. Look for areas you want to play with or areas where you can create some interest with cracks and crevices.

17 APPLY FINAL HIGHLIGHTS

Mix blue, white, red and raw umber to add a final highlight to the places on the mountain where the light is strongest.

18 ADD SHADOWS

Use more of the wash from step 8 to deepen the existing shadowed areas. Notice how the shadowed area directly above the highlight ridge helps to separate and pull the ridge closer to the viewer.

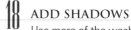

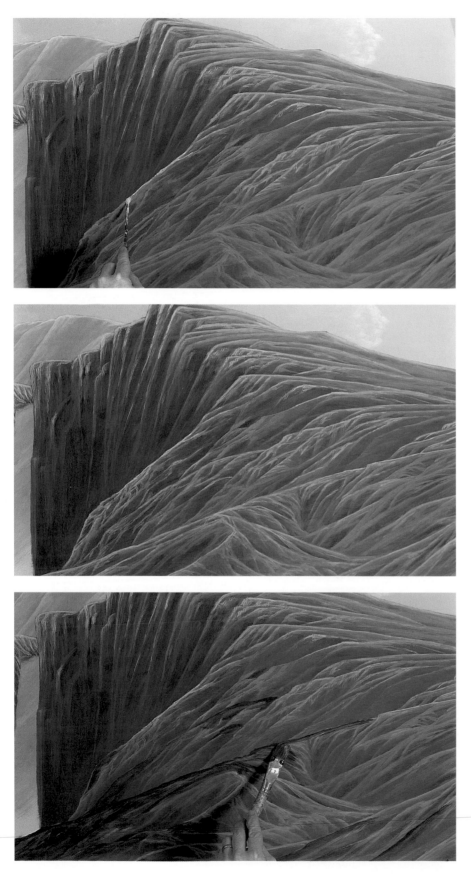

19 ADD ADDITIONAL HIGHLIGHTS

A touch of white can be added to your first highlight color for additional highlights, if necessary.

20 WARM UP THE MOUNTAIN

With your last highlight complete, the mountain has somewhat of a cold and lifeless appearance. You can warm it up with some greenery.

21 BEGIN DEFINING GREEN AREAS

Mix dark blue, raw umber and black to create a rich, dark color that is almost black (pure black is never used because it's too dull and flat). Thin slightly with water so it's somewhat transparent. Lay in this color with a ½-inch (12mm) flat brush, following the contour of the land. This color will be the foundation for the grass.

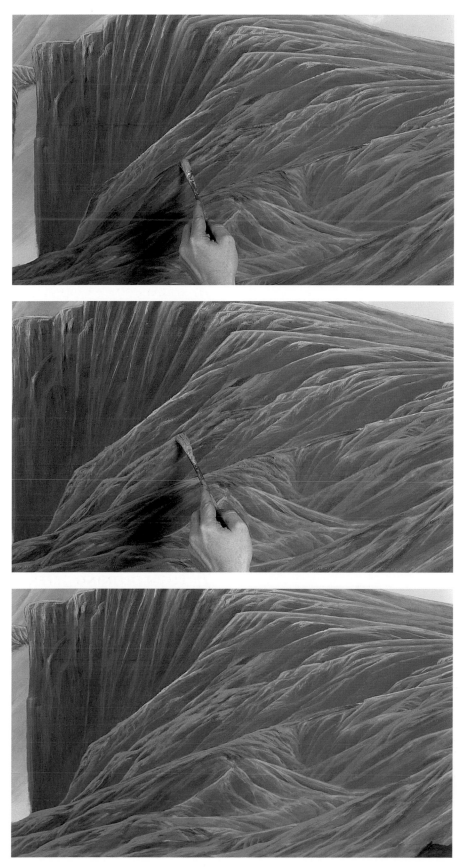

22 PAINT FIRST LAYER OF GRASS

Mix phthalo green and white with your foundation color for the grass color. Be careful not to make it too bright. Using a side-to-side scrubbing motion, lay in color with a ¼-inch (6mm) flat brush following the landscape contours. Allow some of the dark foundation to show. This gives the feel of rough, uneven terrain.

23 HIGHLIGHT GRASS

Highlight again with a mixture of green, raw umber and yellow ochre. If you have too much yellow ochre, the highlight color will be too bright. Knock it down a bit with raw umber.

24 ADD MORE HIGHLIGHTS

An additional highlight can be added if needed by using the second highlight you used on the mountain. Be careful not to overdo it.

25 PAINT THE WATERFALL
If you want to add a waterfall, first paint the blue area for the water. The back of the gorge is where the waterfall will be placed.

26 PAINT REFLECTIONS
Using the same color as the rocks, paint reflections of the rocks in the water, blending the colors and keeping them lower in value than the rocks.

27 ADD THE WATERFALL
Begin laying in the waterfall by mixing a light blue color and warming it up a little with raw umber. Apply this color in long, vertical strokes following the direction and flow of the water. Give the water some movement by painting in some ripples.

28 FINISH THE WATERFALL

Finally, mix a very pale blue, almost white, and use it to highlight the waterfall and ripples in the water. This adds sparkle.

29 PAINT FOREGROUND ROCKS

The foreground in this mural will be rocky terrain with grasses and flowers. When you painted the mountain, you used washes to mute and dull the colors and push them back into the distance. You will want to do the opposite with the foreground. Here the colors will be darker, bolder and brighter because they are closer to the viewer. After drawing in the rocks, base them in with 100 percent coverage using a mix of dark blue, raw umber and a touch of black.

30 SHAPE THE ROCKS
Add enough white to the base mixture to separate the colors and rough in the general shape of the rocks using a ½-inch (12mm) brush. This is similar to step 7.

31 CREATE VARIETY IN THE ROCKS
Using a variety of color mixtures, begin laying in your rocks. Since the rocks are sitting one in front of the other, some rocks are not entirely visible. Starting at the bottom of the mural and working up will make this step easier.

32 ADD HIGHLIGHTS
Highlight your rocks with lighter versions of the color mixtures used for each rock. Build from dark to light as you did for the mountain. Remember your imaginary light source.

33 ADD FOREGROUND GRASS

This rocky terrain is somewhat cold and uninviting. Painting grass between the rocks will add a bit of life and warmth. Because this grass is much closer to the viewer, it will not be painted like the grass you painted earlier. Mix black and red for the base, paint it in and let it dry. Mix black, yellow and a bit of green to make a forest green. Apply in long, sweeping, drybrush strokes using a 2-inch (51mm) chip brush.

34 LAY IN GRASS BLADES

Using the same color and a large liner brush, lay in individual blades of grass, again using quick, sweeping strokes.

35 DEFINE THE GRASS

Mix a grassy green color and use the same liner brush to define the grass blades. Use short, quick strokes in different directions to create the look of clumps of grass.

36 ADD A SPLASH OF COLOR
Mix a brownish orange with yellow, red and brown. Use this color with the liner brush to represent dried blades of grass. This adds an interesting color to the area.

37 APPLY A WASH
To create a sense of depth and a separation between the rows and clumps of grass, make a wash by adding water to the dark base color. Apply the wash to the base of the grass clusters.

38 DEFINE FOREGROUND GRASS
The wash just applied will knock back the taller blades of grass in the clumps closer to the foreground. These areas need to be pumped up again by reapplying the grassy green color that was used earlier.

39 SHARPEN DETAILS
Use the brownish orange color to re-define the dead blades of grass.

The grass is complete. A well-done area of grass with some wildflowers can accent and create interest in a mural.

OPPOSITE PAGE › *This is a flat wall, but a vast sense of depth was created using perspective.*
TOP › *The rocks in the extreme foreground are "real" (three-dimensional replicas). Can you tell where they end and the painted ones begin?*
BOTTOM LEFT › *All the elements in this mural are covered in the step-by-step instructions. Mountain scenes are always a challenge, but satisfying to do.*
BOTTOM RIGHT › *The foreground tree enhances the feeling of depth in this winter scene.*

OPPOSITE PAGE› *The white molding is the only real molding. The rest is a trompe l'oeil mural.*
TOP MIDDLE› *This bedroom wall mural was built up layer by layer. Many elements were painted with a sea sponge.*
TOP RIGHT› *This Ohio River scene almost makes the staircase disappear.*
BOTTOM› *The mural on the right wall was adapted from the Rookwood tile on the left wall.*

Gallery Of Murals

Resources

Books for Further Reading ›
Exploring Color by Nita Leland, North Light
  Books, 1998
Perspective Drawing by Ernest Norling,
  Walter T. Foster Art Books, 1987
*Recipes for Surfaces: Decorative Paint
  Finishes Made Simple* by Mindy Drucker
  and Pierre Finkelstein, Fireside, 1990

Schools ›
Prismatic Painting Studio
Gary Lord and David Schmidt, Directors
935 W. Galbraith Rd.
Cincinnati, OH 45231
Phone/fax 513-931-5520
mhblord@fuse.net

The San Diego School of Decorative Arts
Melanie Royals, Director
2504 Transportation Ave., Ste. H
National City, CA 91950
800-747-9767

Faux Effects, Inc.
Raymond Sandor, Director
3435 Aviation Blvd.
Vero Beach, FL 32960
800-270-8871
Fax 561-778-9653

Sarasota School of Decorative Arts
Susan Sherman and Donna Phelps, Directors
5376 Catalyst Ave.
Sarasota, FL 34233
904-921-6181

Chicago Institute of Decorative Finishing
Kathy Hoette, Director
360 Taft Ave.
Glen Ellyn, IL 60137
800-797-4305
Fax 630-790-4695

The Finishing School
Bob Marx, Director
50 Carnation Ave., Bldg. 2
Floral Park, NY 11001
800-998-3289
Fax 516-327-4853

Definitive Faux Effects
Reohn Zeleznik, Director
7026 Old Katy Rd., Ste. 113
Houston, TX 77024
713-802-9022
Fax 713-802-9021

Ritins Studio, Inc.
170 Wicksteed Ave.
Toronto, Ontario M4G2B6 Canada
416-467-8920
Fax 416-467-8963

Paints ›
Delta Technical Coatings, Inc.
Whittier, CA 90601
562-695-7969
www.deltacrafts.com

Benjamin Moore & Co.
51 Chestnut Ridge Rd.
Montvale, NJ 07645
800-344-0400
www.benjaminmoore.com

Aqua Finishing Solutions
3435 Aviation Blvd.
Vero Beach, FL 32960
800-270-8871
Fax 561-778-9653
www.aquafinishing.com

Brushes ›
Robert Simmons, Inc.
45 W. 18th St.
New York, NY 10011
212-633-9237

Loew-Cornell, Inc.
563 Chestnut Ave.
Teaneck, NJ 07666
201-836-8110
www.loew-cornell.com

Stencils ›
Royal Design Studios
2504 Transportation Ave., Ste. H
National City, CA 91950
800-747-9767
www.aquafinishing.com
/royaldesign.html

Deesigns, Ltd.
147 Jackson St.
Newnan, GA 30264
770-253-6444
Fax 770-253-6466
www.deesigns.com

Dressler Stencil Co.
11030 173rd Ave., S.E.
Renton, WA 98059
425-226-1732
Fax 425-226-3847
www.dresslerstencils.com

The Mad Stencilist
P.O. Box 5497
El Dorado Hills, CA 95762
Phone/fax 916-933-1790
www.madstencilist.com

Organizations ›
Society of Decorative Painters (SDP)
P.O. Box 808
Newton, KS 67114
316-283-9665
www.nstdp.com

Stencil Artisans League, Inc.
526 King St., Ste. 423
Alexandria, VA 22314
703-518-4375
Fax 703-706-9583
www.sali.org

Index